Chag Sameach!

Open this book and let the pages inside
inspire a smile
ignite Jewish pride
teach a lesson or two
enlight and discover
take it all in - from cover to cover.
As you enjoy the Chag from beginning to end
And spend time with family and friends
Remember your Oorah family who cares
And will keep in touch throughout the whole year.

- Rabbi Chaim Mintz

732-730-1000 · OORAH.ORG · THEZONE.ORG · TORAHMATES.ORG · JEWISHLITTLESTAR.ORG

Towards Meaningful Prayer II

Towards Meaningful Prayer II

Inspiring Thoughts & Stories on Tefilah from Classic Sources

by S. Feldbrand

Published by
Lishmoa Lilmod U'lelamed

First edition - First impression / March 2007

Published by **Lishmoa Lilmod U'Lelamed**

Distributed by:
Israel Book Shop
501 Prospect Street
Lakewood, NJ 08701

Tel: (732) 901-3009
Fax: (732) 901-4012
e-mail: isrbkshp@aol.com

ISBN 978-1-60091-022-7

Printed in Canada

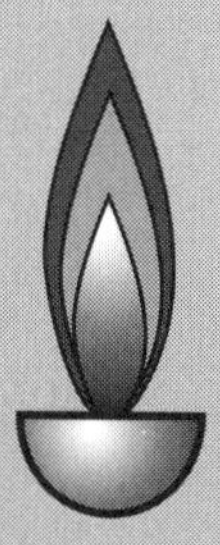

לעילוי נשמת אבי ומורי

ר׳ יהושע אלי׳ בן ר׳ חיים שאול גראסמאן ע״ה

אשר הרבה פעל בהדפסת והפצת ספרים

על טהרת הקדש, ספר זה מוקדש לנשמתו

הטהורה שתעלה מעלה מעלה בגן עדן.

וגם לעילוי נשמת מורי וחמי

ר׳ חיים יהודה בן ר׳ יצחק מאיר ע״ה

דוגמא של עין טובה ורוח נמוכה

ונפש שפלה, שישתשע בנחלי אוהבי יש.

וגם לעילוי כל הנשמות שאין להם מליץ יושר.

תנצב״ה

Tel. 514-276-9886

Rabbi P. Hirschprung
230 Querbes
Montreal, Quebec

I was shown a book in English by Rebbetzin Feldbrand, relating to the topic of tefilah. She has assembled material which is certain to inspire its readers to heightened worship of Hashem, so that they are more acutely aware before Whom they stand in prayer.

The various concepts on the power and importance of tefilah are sure to make prayers more meaningful for all. May Hashem accept our prayers for general and particular salvation.

We should all merit to behold the Bais Hamikdash in its glory, in compassion, speedily in our days.

Translation of Rabbi Hirschprung, Chief Rabbi of Montreal's zt"l approbation to Volume I of "Towards Meaningful Prayer" by Reb. S. Feldbrand.

Table of Contents

PREFACE

This book is for people who want to infuse their prayers with more meaning and heighten their awareness that they are communicating directly with Hashem. Its purpose is to expand our knowledge of the far-reaching effects of our prayer. Keep it handy, and consult it before davening. The techniques recorded in this volume will enable you to summon the wherewithal to daven with renewed focus. For maximum benefit, read no more then a few pages at a time.

No entry is original. I have only collected and translated the words of our Sages, systematizing the material for the reader's benefit as a curator arranges paintings for an exhibit. Mastering its contents will enable you to wield the most potent weapon we have, for survival and spiritual growth. Now, more than ever, we see that "we have no one to rely on but our Father in Heaven," (Sota 9,15). It is therefore imperative that we do everything, in our power, to improve communication with Him. I can only hope that this treasury of thoughts will improve your davening as they have mine. May we thus merit the imminent redemption of our beleaguered people.

ACKNOWLEDGMENTS

I would like to take this opportunity to thank my husband, Rabbi Mayer Feldbrand, for his invaluable help with sources. I would also like to thank my sons, Eliyahu, Eluzar, Mordechai, Shaul, Simcha and Binyamin, for always looking out for seforim and articles on tefillah, which they forwarded to me. May they continue to grow in Torah and Yiras Shamayim.

Once again I would like to express my hakaras hatov to Elky Langer for her highly polished editing of this sefer, and Sury Perl for her professional layout and design. It has been a pleasure working with both of them. Rabbi Moshe Kaufman of Israel Book Shop is always generous with his time and helpful advice, for which I am grateful. My deep gratitude to Haim Sherrf who graciously allowed me once again to use his painting for the book's cover.

I pray that the merit of the great people cited in this work will enable me to complete yet another sefer on this topic, and most importantly, that we all become adept at serving Hashem in a manner that will bring Mashiach, speedily in our days.

S. Feldbrand
Brooklyn, N.Y.

complete, I immediately embarked on collecting material for Volume II. To paraphrase the words of Rav Yisroel Salanter, it was worth all the effort invested in this project to help just one person *daven* once as one should. I know I have benefitted incalculably.

The words of the Maharsham of Brezhan serves as an inspiration to anyone working on a *sefer* of this nature. He writes, "I have been taught in the name of our Rabbis that whoever gathers and organizes the words of our holy books into a new composition is thus forging glorious unifications in the service of Hashem."

The Power of Prayer

Precious Moments

Tefillah is a natural expression of the soul—an essential part of our Jewishness. Communing with the One Who is able to answer our prayers is one of the greatest forms of perfection a person can achieve. In the words of the Rambam's son, Rav Avraham: the moments of the day spent in prayer are "the most precious of which a human being is capable." *Tefillah* infuses all of our deeds with vitality and a deeper sense of our own essence. It polishes and refines all our accomplishments and makes them sparkle with the fire from the deepest recesses of our soul.

Throughout the centuries the Jewish people have repeatedly demonstrated their devotion to *tefillah*. Our Patriarchs, Avraham, Yitzchak and Yaakov, felt the compulsion to pray daily themselves, and then incorporated the practice of regular prayer for their descendants as a basic component of their spiritual arsenal.

What action would their descendants take when faced with trouble? Pray! When the newly liberated Jews were left with no place to run—the Egyptians quickly approaching, wild animals on either side, and the sea ahead—what were they to do? The Torah tells us: "And the Children of Israel cried out to Hashem." As Rashi movingly states, "They embraced the profession of their forefathers, Avraham, Yitzchak and Yaakov," and prayed.

All important endeavors were inaugurated with prayer. In the war against Midyan three thousand soldiers represented each tribe. One thousand fought at the battlefront, another thousand guarded the camp, and the third thousand devoted themselves to prayer (*Bamidbar 22*). In later wars, the King was in charge of praying for the people (*Berachos 4*).

All the miracles performed by the prophets were a result of their prayers. When Yehoshua stopped the sun and Eliyahu and Elisha resurrected the dead, it was not because they were endowed with mysterious, supernatural powers. Their prophetic spirit brought them closer to Hashem so they could pray with greater intensity (*Ramban Devarim 34, 11*).

Hashem's Parting Gift

While prayer has the ability to lift us from the trouble and darkness of this world, prayer is not just something to do when we are in trouble! Prayer fleshes out our identity and infuses our lives with meaning. Nothing in this world measures up to the incomparable sweetness of prayer. It enables us to dedicate ourselves to Hashem; to direct our mind and hearts to His service. Prayer can become a staff of strength for each of us (*Igros Chazon Ish*).

Frequent contact with G-d is of such critical importance that it is Hashem's parting gift to the soul before its descent into this world.

> *A mighty king had an only child he wished to groom as his successor. He called his son and told him that in order to teach him the ropes, he was giving him a position which would enable him to master all aspects of governing his father's far-flung empire. The prince was honored at being given the opportunity to show his mettle. Yet he was distressed that his responsibilities would make it impossible for him to spend time in his father's company as he had in the past. He would miss their frequent, intimate conversations, which had always meant so much to him.*
>
> *When his father saw his son's distress, he expanded the prince's responsibilities to include three personal reports to him daily. This would enable father and son to spend quality time together, helping retain their bond of intimacy.*
>
> *The prince was now delighted with his new assignment. The daily contact with his father would enable the prince to keep the king up-to-date on everything that was happening in his life. When the challenges of his task became*

overwhelming, he could unburden himself to his father, whom he knew would immediately intercede on his behalf. His father was also available to celebrate the joy of accomplishment together with his son. Their daily encounters became the emotional highlight of the prince's day.

The king is Hashem and the prince is the soul. Originally, the soul savored its closeness to Hashem in the world of souls. Ultimately, it was selected for a special mission to this world—to prepare for the eternal bliss in the world to come. Only after accumulating a certain amount of merit can a soul enjoy the endless reward, which awaits it.

The soul relishes the opportunity to serve Hashem and become a part of the holy nation of Klal Yisroel. Yet it is distressed at being separated from its Father in heaven, in Whose presence it has basked until now. Leaving that intimacy behind is very painful. While the ability to rectify numerous worlds, in accordance with Hashem's desire, is a great comfort, the thought of separating from Hashem's presence for many years is daunting.

When Hashem sees the soul's anguish, He gives it the *mitzvah* of prayer to alleviate its sorrow. Three times during the course of the day the soul can speak to its Creator. The soul can articulate all that lies in its heart. It is also an opportune time to make any request and unburden itself. This interaction suffuses the soul's everyday existence with joy.

The knowledge that the soul's connection with Hashem will be maintained and enhanced; that Hashem is always available to provide a listening ear, to aid and comfort the soul, to revel in its joys and to mourn its grief—this is the basis of prayer (*Sichos Be'Avodas Hashem*).

Stirring the Heart

True prayer has been defined as losing one's self in Hashem's presence. It is the activation of the harp that lies within our hearts (*Igros Chazon Ish*). To paraphrase the words of Rav Shimshon Raphael Hirsch, our Divine service requires a clear, enlightened spirit, with a soft, warm heart and the dedicated power of our whole being (*Horev*). Prayer resembles a bow in that the more you pull at it, the greater is its force. The more the heart is stirred, the more energy it releases, boosting our prayers all the way through the heavens (*Shem M'Shmuel, Rosh Chodesh Kislev*).

> *Rav Chaim of Tchernowitz would say that while it is true that there are vast forests where a man can readily go astray, the distance between the mouth and heart is far more substantial. Many are never able to find their way through that huge expanse. They never make the connection from the mouth to the heart (Ha'osher Sheb'tefillah).*

We must continuously lubricate the channels between our hearts and our mouths. This insures that when the opportunity arises and our hearts are galvanized, we will be able to express our feelings through prayer to our Father in Heaven.

Creating Holiness

Prayer has been compared to a ladder (*Zohar 1:226b*). In Yaakov's dream he saw a ladder standing on earth, its top so high that it reached the heavens. Angels were ascending and descending the ladder. The Zohar explains that the angels' ascent alludes to prayer, and the angels' descent refers to Torah study (*Bereishis 28, 12*). Rung by rung, prayer propels man out of the dreariness and darkness of this world, elevating him toward the light of the Infinite (*Torah Or, Vayakhel, p. 88a*). It is the best way to gain entry to the House of Hashem (*Likutei Dibburim*).

Although we would have expected the angels to descend the ladder before ascending, in fact, prayer must come first. With our prayers we lift our base, animal soul from the point of little or no consciousness of G-d to a greater awareness and closeness to Hashem. When the Divine soul communicates with Hashem, even the animal soul becomes filled with holiness. Prayer is a means of elevating our materialism to Hashem, and bringing spirituality down to earth.

The body prays to augment our existence, while the soul prays to transcend existence. Through prayer the body learns the significance of spirituality, and the soul learns that physical existence is also a means of cleaving to Hashem (*Likutei Amarim Tanya 27*).

The people of a certain small town were shocked when their guest, the Baal Shem Tov, insisted on davening in the hall adjacent to the shul, and not inside the regular beis medrash. He chose to daven there because of a moving incident which had occurred one winter day a few years before.

Although the day had been terribly cold—even by Ukrainian standards—the local water carrier had insisted on bringing water to his customers. The freezing weather made the work much slower than usual. After a few hours he was horrified to discover that it was already eleven o'clock in the morning.

"I haven't davened Shacharis yet!" he cried. He raced to shul, where he began putting on his tefilin in the hall. The temperature was so low, though, that the bayis shel yad stuck to his hand. Unwilling to waste even a moment before davening, the water carrier yanked the bayis loose, injuring himself in the process.

The Baal Shem Tov told the townspeople that the water carrier's devotion had cause a great stir in Heaven. It had actually fashioned a new gateway for prayer! The Baal Shem wanted to take advantage of that new approach to heaven, so he decided to pray in the hall, rather than in the shul itself

(Rav Shalom Moskowitz of Shatz, Ohr Ganuz vol. 2, pg. 89).

Spiritual Measure

A person's prayers are a barometer of his spiritual level. The author of the *Chareidim* derives this principle from the verse, "*Metzaref lekesef vekur lezahav veish lefi mehalelo*—the refining pot is for silver and the furnace is for gold, and a man according to his praise." (*Mishlei 27,21*). Just as silver is improved by forging and gold is enhanced in the kiln, so prayer purifies a person's spirit (*Alei Shor*).

Many tend to view prayer as the constant companion of the downtrodden and disheartened. They only invest efforts in their prayers during periods of debility and depression. But this ignores the true function of prayer. Ideally, prayer should be our constant companion, irrespective of whether we are happy or sad; in high periods as well as low periods. *Tefillah* should become the mainstay of our existence, for it is the instrument which insures the fulfillment of our ambitions. We can make use of no better tool to reach our goals.

Rav Yosef Chaim Sonnenfeld was actively involved in overseeing the baking of matzos for Pesach, to ensure that they were strictly kosher and as tasty as possible. One day one of the workers pointed out that another worker was not rolling the dough properly, and thus his matzos were inordinately thick. He felt that a reprimand was in order.

R'Yosef Chaim replied that it would be wrong of him to cause anguish to a poor man because he personally wanted exemplary matzos. "I cannot be a party to that," he exclaimed. "I will daven with all my heart that Hashem should ensure that my matzos are impeccable. I am confident that Hashem will listen to my prayers."

Meaningful Prayer

Only through investing effort in familiarizing ourselves with the different aspects of prayer can we achieve a truly meaningful prayerful experience. If we learn to pray properly, we will derive tremendous pleasure from praying (*Rav Eliyahu Lopian, Lev Eliyahu, vol. I*).

If you feel the pull of a certain phrase while *davening*, slow down and savor it. Let it express your inner feelings and emotions. When a sentence tugs at your heart, let the emotions inundate you until you feel in total unity with the expressed sentiment. These occasional peaks of passion, where words and worshipper fuse together, are the building blocks of good prayer.

During these profound moments of closeness to Hashem we may achieve a glimmer of understanding of the words of the *Chazon Ish*: "When a person is privileged to become aware of the reality of the Almighty's existence, he will experience limitless joy. All the pleasures of the flesh immediately disappear. His soul is enveloped in sanctity; it is as if it has left the body and floats in the upper Heavens. When a person transcends to this level, an entirely new world is open to him. It is momentarily possible for a person to feel like a celestial being. All of the pleasures of this world are as nothing compared to the intense pleasure of a person cleaving to his Creator" (*Emunah U'Bitachon 1, 9*).

Rav Chanoch Henoch of Alexander would say, "The British speak English, the French speak French, the Russians speak Russian. The heart too, has its own language. The language of the heart is prayer" (Ha'osher She'Be'Tefillah).

The Chazon Ish echoed these sentiments: "Any arrangement is acceptable, as long as it flows from the heart" (Igros I, 20).

Greatest of All

The Sefer HaIkarim puts the remarkable power of prayer in perspective. Prayer is one of the commandments; and it is greater than all of them. For prayer saves a person from all possible misfortune, which is not the case with other commandments (*Vani Tefillah - Hakhel*).

As our Sages have said, "*Tefillah* can accomplish more than good deeds. Moshe Rabbeinu had more good deeds to his credit than any other human being, yet he was only granted his request in the merit of his prayers" (*Berachos 32*).

Consider the scope of Moshe Rabbeinu's accomplishments and the merit of his Torah study! He redeemed us from Egypt and enabled the Jewish nation to master the Torah. Yet all these accomplishments played a minor role in his attempts to gain entry to the land. Only the power of his prayer enabled him to receive a view of Eretz Yisrael.

We find in the Midrash that the Jews were saved from Haman not in the merit of their Torah study, but in the merit of their prayers.

> *When Haman's decree was proclaimed, the Torah donned clothes of mourning and raised her voice in wailing before Hashem. The angels joined their cries to hers and called out, "Master of the Universe, if the Jewish people are destroyed, then we are superfluous!"*
>
> *Eliyahu rushed to inform Moshe, "Devoted shepherd, the decree of annihilation has been written and sealed."*
>
> *Moshe asked Eliyahu if there was any leader of stature in the generation.*
>
> *"There is one," Eliyahu replied, "and his name is Mordechai."*
>
> *"Then tell Mordechai what has happened, so he will pray below. Together we will beseech G-d to have compassion on the Jewish people."*

This Midrash demonstrates the unique ability of prayer to save a person from calamity. The merit of Torah study was not enough to save them. Yes, "the study of Torah is equivalent to them all," and its power is unlimited—but when it comes to saving a person from calamity, nothing beats prayer (*Or Yechezkel p. 195*).

Prayer can also be more effective than good deeds. Rav Aharon Kotler adds that *tefillah* can achieve results in situations where good deeds fail. Even if a person is undeserving, his prayer can still accomplish a great deal. Hashem empowered prayer to open the channels of largesse and compassion for humanity (*Mishnas Reb Aharon Tefillah, 1*).

Annulling Decrees

The miracle of Purim teaches us that prayer and repentance can open all doors and tear all decrees asunder (*Bais Avraham in the name of Harav Hakadosh of Berditchev*).

Even after a decree is finalized, it is possible to annul it with prayer (*Rosh Hashanah 16*). *Tefillah* is so powerful that it can change nature, save a person from danger and invalidate a guilty verdict (*Rabbeinu Bachya on Tefillah*).

A person should feel confident that prayer said properly can overturn a negative verdict. If a person is in terrible straits, or if he has a sick relative, he should go to a Rav and learn the proper way to *daven* and plead for compassion (*Meiri Bava Basra 117*).

The Gemara suggests that only the prayer of a multitude can revoke a decree that has been finalized (*Rosh Hashanah 18*). The Ikarim maintains that this applies to a decree finalized with an oath. Only a huge number of people can reverse this type of judgment, for Hashem never rejects the prayers of scores of people (*Berachos 8*).

When Rav David Luria, known as the Radal, was a young child, it was clear to all that he was destined for greatness. At age five he had mastered all of Tanach, including the principles of grammar and the holy tongue. At six he was swimming in the sea of the Talmud with a great scholar selected by his father to study with him. By age nine he knew the first nine tractates of Shas by heart.

The local poretz heard about this wunderkind and expressed the desire to meet him. At the meeting was a math professor from France, who had been hired to teach the landowner's children. The poretz was so impressed by the child's knowledge that he was determined to have the professor study with the child an hour each day, so he could acquire secular wisdom.

When the child was informed of the landowner's decision, he spent the entire night crying out to Hashem not to deprive him of an hour of learning, which he had reserved for review. In the morning it was discovered that the teacher had been accidentally killed (Raboseinu She'bagolah).

One Rosh Hashanah in World War I, Russian soldiers surrounded the synagogue plaza in Mir looking for draft evaders. Among the shuls located in the plaza was the Yeshiva Minyan. All those praying there were draft evaders. The panic was acute. The young men were in imminent danger of being seized and sent straight to the front.

An intense discussion ensued to determine the next step. It was suggested that they mingle with the others praying in the nearby synagogues where they would not be as conspicuous.

The Mashgiach, R' Yerucham Levovitz, insisted that they continue to pray together. He reassured them that Hashem would miraculously save them. Their prayers took on a greater intensity. In the end, the soldiers thoroughly searched all the other shuls in the plaza—but never crossed the threshold of the Yeshiva Minyan (Rabbi Shlomo Wolbe).

Turning to Hashem

On Rosh Hashanah Hashem designates a measure of prosperity for the Jewish people. This prosperity is in the form of a sound that has not yet been articulated. When does Hashem allow it to take on its final shape? The Kedushas Levy explains that Hashem waits for our input. Our daily prayers are required for the designated prosperity to reach us. Why is this necessary? Because we are beloved by Hashem, and He wishes to hear our voices. He therefore arranges matters so we will turn to Him constantly (*Kedushas Levy, Rosh Hashana*).

The world has been arranged so that every aspect of our existence hinges on prayer. Since no endeavor can succeed without prayer, we must constantly thank Hashem for the past and petition Him for the future. Communing with Hashem is our first recourse and our last resort. Man must always turn to Hashem to request his needs. If a person is not motivated to pray, Divine assistance will never reach him (*Derech Hashem on Prayer 4, 3*).

The verse, "And I will conceal and hide my face on that day" (*Devarim 31:18*), is explained by the Vilna Gaon as referring to a lack of understanding on the part of the Jewish people. They do not appreciate that suffering has come upon them because Hashem has hidden from them. Hashem wants us to seek Him out by taking advantage of the ultimate weapon—prayer (*Divrei Eliyahu Parshas Va'Yelech*).

Our sages inform us (*Nidah 70*), that if a person wishes to attain wisdom, wealth, or male offspring, he should seek compassion from He Who is Master of wisdom, wealth and children. The Torah does not advocate the pursuit of traditional methods to reach these goals. Natural methods often fail. The most important effort we must make is prayer.

The same applies to everything we seek to accomplish in this world. We must make use of our *siddur* and *Tehillim* for all our endeavors. Even the most mundane activities should be preceded by prayer, bolstered with prayer and concluded with prayer.

The Baal Shem Tov asked a disciple to take on the task of closely guarding the production of wine, from the harvest of the grapes through the finished product. Reb David of Mikolayev set out in late summer and spent over two months ensuring the highest standards of kashrus in the wine manufacturing. He stood over the trappers in the vats and protected the wine from harm on the road home. But all his work and travails came to naught when a non-Jewish Cossack helped himself to some wine right after he arrived back in Mezibuzh.

Reb David was devastated. He had invested so much effort in the wine, and now it had become unfit! He asked the Baal Shem Tov to explain why Hashem had rejected his heartfelt endeavor.

The Baal Shem Tov explained that he had devoted too much energy to guarding the wine, leaving no room for Hashem's help. "You should have invested greater effort in davening to Hashem that He stand at your side and watch over the wine." (Baal Tzror Chaim in the name of his father, Baal Shem Tov on the Torah)

Sometimes even the shortest prayers from the most

assimilated Jew, uttered as a last resort, can have a tremendous impact.

Near the end of World War II, three Hungarian Jews were determined to escape a German labor camp and reach the presumably friendlier arms of the approaching Russians, before the Germans attempted to destroy all traces of their heinous deeds.

In the confusion engendered by the approaching forces, they were able to escape to the nearby forest. They knew they didn't have much time until their disappearance was discovered and the pursuit would begin. They ran, pushing themselves as long as their strength held out, moving in the direction of the Russians.

Suddenly they heard frightening sounds in the distance—the sound of barking dogs. The Germans were after them, and they knew they would never be able to outrun their pursuers on foot. Instead, they quickly climbed as high as they could into three nearby tall trees.

Moments later, German soldiers with whips and dogs came into view. With the help of Hashem neither soldiers nor animals noticed the escapees as they whipped past their trees and continued deeper into the forest.

Shaking with fear at their close call, they hoped the Nazis would not risk pursuing them too deeply into a forest where encounters with the advancing Soviet troops was a real possibility. After an hour they were relieved to see the Nazis and their beasts heading back in the direction of the camp.

When all was quiet, they descended from the trees and resumed their trek deep into the forest. As the sun began to rise, they found a well-hidden pit where they curled up and slept. For three days they traveled at night and collapsed into a concealed area at night.

On the fourth day they spotted a house in a clearing. They waited, watching carefully until it became apparent that the house was abandoned. They climbed up to the roof and made themselves mattresses of straw. In a short time all three were sound asleep.

They woke to the sound of the door crashing loudly open from a kick. If it was the Germans, they were doomed. If it was the Russians, they tended to shoot first and ask questions later.

Someone screamed, "Shema Yisrael!" A quick order was barked in Russian. Three Russian soldiers led by an officer appeared in their line of vision. The muzzles of soldiers' rifles were aimed directly at them, but they did not shoot.

Later the passage of events was sorted out. One of the three hidden men had instinctively shouted Shema Yisrael. The commanding officer of the Russian patrol was a Jew.

When he heard "Shema Yisrael," he had roared the command, "Hold your fire!"

A completely non-religious assimilated Jew, whose father had been a non-Jew, had instinctively cried out "Shema Yisrael". It was that prayer which saved their lives (Kfar Chabad Magazine, Sichos Ha'Shavuah # 604).

Always Answered

When Hashem said to Moshe, "Release me, and I shall destroy them" (*Devarim 9:14*), it was a signal to future generations that prayer was exceptionally powerful. Moshe's prayers "prevented" Hashem from destroying the Jewish people.

Every time we pray, it should be with the certain knowledge that Hashem definitely responds. This is the basis of addressing Hashem as "*Shomeah tefillah*—listening to our prayers"—a true blessing which is rooted in fact. We ask Hashem to listen, and then thank Him for doing so. We are certain, without doubt, that He answers us each and every time (*Igeres Ha'Teshuvah Chapter 11*).

The Yerushalmi tells of a young Jewish boy traveling alone on a ship when a ferocious storm broke out. The entire boat was full of pagans. With the boat about to capsize, everyone called out to his god to save them. Only the Jewish boy did nothing, until the others urged him to call out to his G-d,

Who is known to answer those who call out to Him. The child davened to Hashem, and the seas immediately calmed.

When they anchored ashore, the gentiles asked the Jewish boy why he did not join them on their shopping expedition. "I am alone and forlorn," he replied. The gentiles vehemently denied his assertion: "How could anyone who saw his prayers answered feel lonesome?" (Berachos 9)

The non-Jews understood the significance of a simple Jewish prayer—the prayer of a Jewish child, who was praying on his own on an ordinary day. He was not a Torah scholar. He was not in the company of other Jews, which would have added the merit of *davening* with others. Yet still, his prayer achieved results.

The Chofetz Chaim writes that we are obligated to believe that Hashem will respond to our prayers for personal deliverance in the twinkling of an eye (*Machaneh Yisrael 2:20*). Inherent in our obligation to anticipate our imminent redemption is the assurance of personal salvation.

Pressberg, home of the yeshiva of the Chasam Sofer, was also the location for the king's coronation. On one occasion, King Ferdinand's coronation was scheduled for Yom Kippur. The Chasam Sofer was deeply distressed. He sensed that many Jews would desecrate that holy day in their desire to take part in the festivities. The leaders of the Jewish community tried to postpone the event, but they were not successful.

The Chasam Sofer turned to his prayers. On the day before Yom Kippur he did not come home from shul, and continued to pray until noon. As he finished praying, black clouds filled the sky. A heavy downpour arrived, complete with gale force winds. The coronation was postponed (Olamo Shel Abbah).

When Rebbe Nachman of Breslov was young he indulged in all types of ascetic behavior. Later he regretted his asceticism. "If I had known the power of prayer I would not have bothered with any austere measures. I would simply have prayed day and night—for through prayer, everything can be achieved" (Sheifos p. 235).

Prayer is our most powerful weapon. A person's money, wisdom and strength are not as effective as his prayers (*Shochar Tov ch. 142*). Why is Yaakov compared to a worm? (*Yeshaya 41:14*) Just as the worm's mouth provides sustenance and protection, so is prayer our ultimate purveyor and defense. Even though the worm is a soft creature it can fell the mightiest cedars with its mouth. The Jewish people can similarly make use of prayer to reach their challenging goals (*Midrash Tanchuma Beshalach 9*).

Anyone who underestimates prayer's power will be unable to exploit its might. Even if a person deserves health, safety, or comfort—even if it is all prepared for him—he will not receive it unless he prays for it. In addition, prayer enables us to obtain that which we do not deserve—including items that we would never even dream of obtaining.

The verse in *Eicha* (*3:60*) that suggests that when a person prays with intensity for something that is not beneficial for him, Hashem must create a barrier to prevent the prayers from ascending to Heaven (*Kol Dodi Dofek*). For there is always the chance that when we pray for something harmful, our prayers may still be answered!

Tefillah is so powerful that Hashem does not reject the petition of the wicked. When the wicked pray, Hashem must make the extra effort, as it were, to avoid the receipt of their prayers (*Binah Le'itim Derush 62*).

> *One who commits unintentional manslaughter is exiled to a city of refuge until the Kohen Gadol dies. The Gemara says that the mother of the Kohen Gadol used to send gifts to these people so they would not pray that her son should die.*
>
> *What if they do pray? Will the prayers of those who have taken the life of another person have any effect? The Talmud Bavli explains that the Kohen Gadol is in danger because he is culpable for each accidental killing. Had he prayed that the Jewish people be spared any homicides, perhaps this crime would not have taken place.*

This demonstrates the great power of prayer, writes Rav Meir

Bergman. While a person is responsible for his own deeds, another person's prayer can rescue him from wrongdoing. Indeed, the Talmud Yerushalmi takes the power of prayer even further, noting that the murderer's prayer is a threat to the Kohen Gadol because even when a wicked person prays for something that is objectively wrong, he may still be answered.

How can this be? R' Bergman explains (based on a comment of the Maharsha to Kiddushin 29b) that it is one of the laws of nature that prayer is answered. No special Divine intervention is required! Hashem has programmed the laws of nature to respond to our prayers (*Sha'arei Orah vol. II*).

A baal teshuva named Rabbi Baruch Hyman, a true G-d fearing Jew who became a very successful lecturer, once revealed the reason for his success.

When Ben-Gurion was Prime Minister of Israel, the Minister of Education, Zalman Aran, admired him tremendously. Although Aran was not a religious Jew, his wife maintained a traditional Jewish home and she always lit the Shabbos candles. Knowing the power of prayer, she would pray that her children become great people. Since her husband always praised Ben-Gurion highly, she would pray that her children become great—as Ben-Gurion.

Ben-Gurion once went to visit the Chazon Ish in Bnei Brak. After the meeting, Ben-Gurion told to Zalman Aran how impressed he had been by the greatness of the Chazon

Ish. He admitted that he felt himself to be in the presence of an angel.

Aran told his wife about the great impact the Chazon Ish had had on his boss. She listened to his words attentively. From then on she decided to pray that her children should grow up and become great—as the Chazon Ish. After all, if Ben-Gurion, whom her husband regarded so highly, was so impressed by the Chazon Ish, then surely she should go for the best.

Rabbi Hyman was the grandson of Zalman Aran. The prayers of his grandmother had its effect after many years, despite the fact that she wasn't particularly righteous. As Rabbi Hyman put it, "It brought me close to Torah and mitzvos and enabled me to succeed in my spiritual endeavors."

In *Tehillim* (*34:16-18*) we recite, "The eyes of Hashem are in the direction of the righteous, and His ears [attuned] to their cry. The face of Hashem is against evildoers, to cut off their memory from earth. They cried out and Hashem heeds, and from all their troubles He rescues them." According to the Ibn Ezra and Metzudas David, "they" in the last verse refers to the evildoers who were mentioned in the previous verse. Even though they are evildoers and Hashem wants to "cut off their memory from earth," if they return to Hashem and cry out to Him, He will listen.

The Gemara informs us that when Rebbe passed away, his disciples declared that whoever revealed that he had died would be stabbed. The Shita Mekubetzes offers the following eye-opening explanation for this harsh proclamation: "The power of tefillah is so great that even after Rebbe's death, his disciples could have brought him back to life with their prayers. Once his death became common knowledge, however, special intervention would have been required to perform a public miracle. Therefore, anyone who revealed his death made Rebbe's death an irreversible finality, and was deserving of being stabbed" (Alenu Le'Shabeach, Vayikra p. 228).

A person stands before Hashem, knowing that he is helpless when left to his own devices—only Hashem can help him. This *tefillah* will undoubtedly make an impression in Heaven. Genuine effort to instill our prayers with warmth, while placing all our trust and faith in the Creator of the world, will result in Hashem demonstrating that we were right in trusting in Him.

Perhaps someone will whisper to you, "Do you really think we can accomplish what our fathers and grandfathers accomplished with their prayers? Hashem answered their prayers and saved them from calamities and misfortune because of their lofty stature. We are on such a low spiritual level—our *tefillos* surely don't have such power or value!"

Do not listen to these false arguments! Our sages teach us, "Yiftach in his generation is equal to Shmuel in his generation."

Each generation is judged by its own criteria. Even today, a person can obtain prosperity directly from Hashem's hand and experience miracles.

The Zohar explains that waters of the flood are called the "waters of Noach" because Noach did not pray adequately on behalf of his generation. By inference we learn that if he had prayed sufficiently, he would have succeeded in reversing the decree. The Kedushas Levi, the Chassam Sofer and others point out that the quality of his prayers was deficient because he did not believe that they were powerful enough to avert the flood. This lack of faith weakened their impact.

In the battle against Amalek, the verse informs us that Moshe Rabbeinu enabled the Jews to overpower the Amalekites by raising his hands aloft. As long as they gazed upward they prevailed. The Torah tells us, "*Va'yehi yadav emunah*, and his hand remained faithful," which Targum translates as "his hands were outstretched in prayer." The Sefas Emes explains the use of the word "faithful": Moshe Rabbeinu had faith that his prayer would achieve results, and therefore they succeeded (*Sichos Hischaskus, Devarim p. 19*).

The Gemara describes the scenario of Reuven the farmer who rented a piece of land from his friend Shimon and agreed to split the profits. If there was a locust attack or a drought or flood, which could not have been prevented, then they would both absorb the non-preventable loss.

One fall Shimon took Reuven to court, claiming that he had demonstrated negligence by planting barley instead of wheat. Reuven could not understand what difference it made. The barley had been growing beautifully, but then a flood destroyed the crop—a catastrophe that could not have been avoided. But Shimon insisted that if he had known that Reuven would plant barley, he would have prayed that the field of barley should thrive. He hadn't known that Reuven had changed the crop, and he instead prayed for the wheat to thrive. Shimon insisted that the change was neglectful, because it rendered his prayers ineffective.

The Gemara concludes that Shimon was right. Reuven was remiss in not informing Shimon of the change (Bava Metzia 106).

Rav Shlomo Eiger once wrote to his father, Rav Akiva Eiger, asking him to daven for a sick woman named Sara bas Rivka. Rav Akiva wrote back, "I davened for Sara bas Rivka and was not answered. Perhaps there is a mistake in the names?"

Rav Shlomo asked the woman's husband, and sure enough, the woman's name was Rivka bas Sara. He wrote to his father again, and soon the response came back, "I davened for Rivka bas Sara and was answered." The woman indeed recovered (Meisharshav Esh Lohet, 5760 vol. 2, p. 147).

One who does not believe that his prayer is worthy of acceptance is considered a man of little faith.

The Gemara informs us that a person who raises his voice while praying is a man of little faith (Berachos 24b). Rashi explains that the Gemara is referring to a person who raises his voice because he doesn't believe that Hashem listens to quiet prayer.

When a person's faith is incomplete, he may try to compensate by raising his voice, believing that this way his prayer will have a better chance at being heard. He believes that Hashem is ignoring him, and if he raises his voice, he will manage arouse Hashem's mercy. Such a person is therefore considered a man of little faith (Sefer Ha'Zichronos).

The Chazon Ish wrote, "Using *tefillah*, every person has the ability to attain that which is good." (*Igros 1, 1*). In another letter he writes, "In times when mishaps occur, I grasp firmly to the belief that nothing is left to chance; rather, all is from Hashem. I pray intently that the decree should be rescinded" (*Igros I, 132*).

In his youth, Rav Yaakov Dovid Weintraub of Radomsk was once pouring out his heart to the Alexander Rebbe. "Why are you concerned?" the Rebbe asked. "You have a close acquaintance who will look after everything for you!"

Seeing Rav Yaakov Dovid's puzzled expression, the Rebbe

explained, "Hashem is near to all who call out to Him—to all who call out to Him in truth. I believe that you are among those who call out to Hashem sincerely."

Years later, in his great work on Tehillim, Rav Yaakov Dovid describes the tremendous power of prayer, even when it comes from "a simple person like me."

To prove his point, Rav Yaakov Dovid tells the following story:

"A man living in the village of Wolko, which is quite a distance from Radomsk, once owed me a large sum of money, and I decided to travel to him to collect the debt. I began my trek to Wolko dressed in summer clothing. Along the way the weather turned unseasonably cold and rainy. I had asked for directions to Wolko, but somehow got lost in a field. I had no idea which way to turn. On one side of the field was a forest, and on the other a river.

"I stood in the pouring rain. Every minute in the freezing cold was a real threat to my life. I knew that if I was forced to spend the night there, there was no natural way that I could survive. I began to pour out my heart to the Ribono Shel Olam, 'Please, Hashem, Master of the world, don't take my life from me here! Please show me the way out!'

"When I finished my short prayer a bird appeared suddenly, flying just a few feet above the ground. I knew in

my heart that the bird was a messenger from heaven, sent to show me the way. I followed it all the way to the village, and then it flew away" (Marbitzei Torah Me'Olam HaChassidus).

Changing Nature

Prayer is both a force of nature and a very powerful means of modifying nature. The grass did not grow until Adam prayed, to indicate that prayer is as vital to photosynthesis as rain and sunshine. Prayer transports all aspects of nature to its final stages (*Introduction to Tefilas Channah*).

Not only does prayer facilitate nature; it can also change nature. This is a basic principle of our faith (*Otzar Tefilos Yisrael*).

Someone once sought the Chazon Ish's counsel in a difficult matter. Expressing his reservations for success in his endeavor, the man employed a Talmudic expression, "Lav bechol yoma esrachesh nisa—miracles do not occur every day" (Pesachim 50a). Retorted the Chazon Ish: "No! Bechol yoma esrachesh nisa! Miracles do occur every day!"

Someone is drowning. There is no life preserver to throw him, no boat, no telephone—and no one can swim there to help him. Do not conclude that there is nothing to be done to save him! We all possess the means of rescuing the man. Prayer has a manifest practical effect! (*Chazon Ish, Emunah U'Bitachon*) The worst diagnosis voiced by doctors should not shatter a person's equilibrium. Optimism is still appropriate (*Ibid, correspondence 126*).

The Chazon Ish explained that prayer works miracles in medicine as well. He writes to a childless couple, "When a doctor decides there is no possibility of you having children—his assessment means nothing. There is still hope, and may Hashem bless you with children" (*Kovetz Igros I; 115*).

Doctors were given the power to heal, but not to pass sentence. Prayers can open all doors and ascend on high to affect a complete rescue.

In the city of Posen a Jew was suffering from a very rare disease. When R' Akiva Eiger learned that the king's physician was in town, he asked him to examine the sick man.

The physician's verdict was that the disease had no cure. "If the king had the disease," R' Akiva asked, "would you so quickly have despaired of restoring him to health?"

The physician thought for a moment. "In fact, the king did suffer once from this very same ailment. There was a medicine that saved his life—but it was very difficult to acquire. There is a very rare bird that lives in a distant land, which is difficult to trap. Only its flesh can heal the illness.

"The king, with his army and flotilla of ships, was able to send a contingent of soldiers to capture the rare bird. But a commoner doesn't have the same resources, and would not be successful in acquiring the bird."

R' Akiva Eiger went home and prayed, "Master of the Universe, your sons are also kings, and the sons of kings! And now, one of Your sons needs help. He needs that rare bird. Send her to us."

A short while later R' Akiva heard a tapping at the window. The window was opened, and a strange bird flew in. R' Akiva gave orders that it should be cooked and fed to the sick man. R' Akiva kept only the bird's wings. After eating the flesh of the bird, the man recovered.

When the king's physician was once again in town R' Akiva sent him the bird's wings. The doctor exclaimed, "Only a Jew could bring about such a miracle!"

A granddaughter of Rabbi Chaim Moshe Mandel suffered from an ongoing migraine. For weeks she was in excruciating pain; despite her grandfather's numerous blessings, nothing seemed to help.

The young woman underwent numerous medical tests, hoping that the doctors would be able to diagnose the problem. In the meantime, she continued to suffer on a daily basis.

Her husband was beside himself. Feeling utterly lost, he went to Rabbi Chaim Moshe Mendel once again. "There's only so much a person can deal with!" he cried to his wife's grandfather. "It's too much already!"

R' Chaim Moshe shuddered at the pain in his cry. "We must put everything aside and beseech Hashem for her recovery," he declared.

He took two books of Tehillim from the bookshelf and gave one to his rebbetzin. The two went into the shul and stood beside the Aron HaKodesh. Rabbi Chaim Moshe prayed in one corner and the rebbetzin in the other, just like Yitzchak and Rivkah, crying to Hashem as they recited chapters of Tehillim.

The next morning, the young woman who had been so severely afflicted awoke early. She felt a little unusual. She rubbed her head—and then realized what had changed: the headache was gone! "I was born again!" she shouted with joy. "I feel like a new person!" Miraculously, her migraine had simply disappeared.

When the results of her tests arrived, they indicated that she had been suffering from bacteria that had spread across her skull. The only way to treat this affliction was with high doses of antibiotics. In the young woman's case, however, the symptoms had simply disappeared, thanks to the impassioned prayers of her righteous grandparents (Her'ah L'anav).

An X-ray indicated that a certain individual was stricken with a dreaded disease. A subsequent X-ray showed no sign of illness. Rav Yehudah Zev Segal, the Manchester Rosh Yeshivah, commented, "The first x-ray was not wrong—it was the power of prayer which caused the illness to disappear."

A little boy with a dreaded illness had to undergo difficult treatments that would cure him, with Hashem's help. The boy's parent had spoken to him before the first treatment and explained that the medicine which would make him get well would cause unpleasant side effects. When they told him that he would lose his hair, he turned to the wall and cried out, "Ribbono shel Olam! I believe that all You do is for the good, as my parents have taught me. I know that losing my hair will cause me embarrassment, but that doesn't bother me. But Ribbono shel Olam, please help me so my payos will not fall out. A Yid has to have payos!"

He burst into tears and continued to pray for a long time, with his parents crying at his side.

After the treatments, the father took his child to Rav Chaim Kanievsky. "Look, wonder of wonders! My son's tefillos were answered and his payos remained!" (Aleinu Le'Shabeach)

It appears that when a supernatural event occurs as a result of our prayers, it is not considered a miracle. The Maharsha derives this principle from the story of Rav Acha and the demon. Abaye had Rav Acha sleep in the Bais Midrash despite the dangerous demon who frequented that particular shul. He relied on Rav Acha's piety to save him from harm. Abaye was certain that Rav Acha's prayers would form a protective shield around him, without the need for miraculous intervention. Abaye would never have opted for a supernatural tactic that might diminish Rav Acha's merits (*Maharsha Kiddushin 29*).

Beyond Barriers

What happens to our prayers when we have created monumental barriers with our sins? We must burrow beneath the barriers. Even if these barriers are forged from the sturdiest material, it is always possible to dig a passageway beneath them.

The best example of this is with Menashe, king of Yisrael. Menashe placed a four-faced idol in the Bais Hamikdash, ensuring that whichever direction people entered, they would see and worship it (*Devarim Rabbah 2,20*). He promulgated idol worship throughout the length and breath of Eretz Yisroel.

Captured by the Assyrians, Menashe was subject to savage and barbaric torture. One by one he called out to his idols, begging for mercy—but his pleas went unheeded. Finally, he remembered the G-d of his fathers (*Yerushalmi Sanhedrin 10,2 Melachim II, 20, Divrei Ha'yamim II, 33*).

The Gemara informs us that he made his heart subservient to Hashem (*Sanhedrin 10, 2*). Hashem then created a tunnel to allow Menashe's supplication to reach His Throne and save him. It was only due to his excessive deference that Hashem respond to his prayers (*Nesivos Shalom, Toldos*).

The definition of a "tunnel prayer" is to beg and plead with Hashem until He has compassion on us. When we are girded with faith, these prayers take on additional muscle, enabling them to rise heavenward. The ladder "inclined toward the ground" in Yaakov's dream (*Bereishis 28:12*) symbolizes the natural order of Hashem's interaction with us, which is launched on *Rosh Hashanah.* Yet the verse informs us that Hashem's presence hovered over the ladder. This symbolizes Hashem's availability, beyond the scope of the ordinary and pre-ordained—allowing life-transforming prayer to shatter all barriers (*Toras Avos, Vayetzeh*).

When a person screams and cries to the point of exhaustion, this heartfelt prayer is never rejected. A fervent cry reverses even a deep-rooted decree (*Zohar, Shemos*). Keep praying from day to night until Hashem provides relief (*Oros Eilim*).

A man was married for many years without children. One evening he visited a great rabbi who seemed to suggest that he should come to terms with his childlessness. He felt as if his heart had broken in two. He immediately went to Chevron where he prayed with all his might, crying and screaming without stop, pleading and begging. People at the scene joined in his tears. Within ten months he had a son (Hischazkua Be'tefillah La'Hashem).

Our sages counsel us to brace ourselves when we pray—suggesting that there are obstacles that we must overcome (*Berachos 32*). Their language implies confidence that all impediments, even those ordained by the laws of nature, can be overcome by prayer (*Nesivos Olam, Nesiv Derech Eretz, ch. 1*).

Hashem gave our Matriarchs years of childlessness so their prayers would construct a conduit for the future. Through prayer, their nature was changed, and they became capable of having children. Later generations would benefit from their prayers (*Imrei Pinchas, Lech Lecha*). The Toldos Yaakov Yosef points out that once nature had been changed to accommodate a miracle, it then became an established phenomenon (*Tzav p. 289*). Our forefathers enabled their children's prayers to modify nature.

Hashem continues to harness nature on our behalf. It is an eternal commitment. When natural channels are blocked, each of us has the ability to take advantage of supernatural channels forged by our forefathers (*Hischazkus Be'tefillah La'Hashem p.*

41). When we see the effectiveness of our prayers in seemingly insurmountable situations, we experience firsthand the power of prayer to circumvent nature (*Alei Shor vol. 2*).

The prayers of our Patriarchs and Matriarchs also ensured that their descendants would endure as a sheep among seventy wolves, without being devoured. Our ability to persevere against all odds is another aspect of their prayerful legacy (*Kovetz Sichos of R' Nosson Wachtfogel*).

Maximum Results

Most of us tend to make do with partial reprieves in response to our prayers. It is unfortunate that people are satisfied with limited results, without pushing for a comprehensive salvation (*Tzidkas Ha'Tzadik, 213*).

When we pray, we do the equivalent of grabbing hold, as it were, of Hashem. This is why Hashem said to Moshe Rabbeinu, "Leave me be" (*Shemos, 32*). This applies to Moshe Rabbeinu, to the Jewish people as a whole, and to each individual (*Kemotzeh Shalal Rav, Devarim, pp. 306-397*). We must pray with persistence, allowing no possibility of non-compliance (*Temurah 16*). We must pray for the maximum—though always with the postscript, "Only if it is in our best interest."

Chana's prayer is an example of this type of prayer. She requested that Hashem give her the seed of men. R' Yochanan explains that she was asking for a child equal to two men, referring to Moshe and Aharon.

Chana was not satisfied with a son who would be a scholar, who would fear G-d, who was righteous and pious. She was not content with a son like Moshe Rabbeinu, who was the instrument for the giving of the Torah. Nor was she content with a son like Aharon, who wore the breastplate, entered the Holy of Holies, and in whose merit the Jews were protected by the clouds of glory. She wanted a son who would equal both Moshe and Aharon. She therefore merited giving birth to Shmuel, who was the equivalent of them both (*Hischazkus Be'Tefillah La'Hashem*).

> *Rebbe Nachman was once asked for guidance in choosing the best method to achieve closeness to Hashem.*
>
> *"Study Torah" the Rebbe advised.*
>
> *"I am incapable," the questioner replied.*
>
> *"Then daven!" Rebbe Nachman advised. "Through prayer one can accomplish everything. All that is good becomes accessible, including Torah, service of Hashem and holiness. Nothing in the universe is withheld" (Hishtapchus Ha'Nefesh 12).*

On Behalf of Others

Pray for your neighbor first, writes Rav Avraham Abele of Gombin (Magen Avraham 130:2). When we hear of the suffering of others, our hearts should melt into prayer.

> *A blind man made the effort to attend the funeral of Rav Chaim Shmulevitz. When he was asked about his relationship with the deceased, he retold the following incident: "When Rav Chaim heard that my doctors had despaired of my ability to see again, he burst into tears which lasted for twenty minutes" (Siach Yisrael).*

How is it possible to turn back to everyday matters when we have just heard that a fellow Jew is in distress? The only way to relieve the pain weighing us down is to turn to the ultimate Healer and pray on behalf of our friend.

> *Rav Chaim Kanievsky told the following remarkable story about his grandfather, Rav Aryeh Levine:*
>
> *Rav Aryeh collected large amounts of funds, which he secretly channeled, to many widows, orphans and needy individuals. In the month of Nissan the indigents he had taken under his wing were in very desperate straits. The money they received from Rav Aryeh enabled them to buy food for Pesach.*
>
> *A large number of philanthropists, knowing of his*

devotion to the poor and downtrodden, happily entrusted tzedakah funds to Rabbi Levine. He was thus spared the embarrassment associated with soliciting funds—until one Nissan, during World War I. The war had taken its toll on the community, and while the need was greater than usual, donations were far skimpier. Rabbi Levine found himself going from door to door begging for funds. Unfortunately, he met with little success.

He went to the Kosel to pour his heart out to Hashem on behalf of His needy children. For an hour he beseeched Hashem to provide the funds needed to enable his clients to receive the basics for the coming Pesach. As Rav Aryeh moved away from the Kosel an unknown Arab thrust a parcel wrapped in newspaper into his hands, and then disappeared. In the parcel was the exact amount of money he usually distributed before Pesach.

"It is our family's belief," R'Chaim is quick to add, "that the Arab was Eliyahu the prophet" (Aleinu Le'Shabeach, Vayikra).

Take note of the power of prayer on behalf of others, and use it well! When Hagar conceived, people began looking down on Sarai, thinking that Hagar was more virtuous since she had conceived almost immediately. Sarai complained to Avraham, "*Chamasi alecha*, my suffering is due to you!" (*Bereishis 6:5*). It had become apparent that Avraham had been praying that he be blessed with a child—but hadn't emphasized that he and Sarai have one together. Why did Sarai describe her husband's neglectfulness as "*chamas*", a term usually used for theft? Rav Shach suggests that Sarai understood that to withhold or even neglect to pray for someone you can help is tantamount to robbery.

Every word in the Torah is full of lessons for us. Here, Sarah Imeinu teaches us that when we *can* help, we *must* help! It is imperative that we take a *siddur* in hand and pray. Not doing so is equivalent to snatching the salvation of another person out of their hands (*Merosh Amana*). If a person has the opportunity to pray for another and does not do so, he is called a sinner (*Berachos* 12b).

> *Rabbi Yaakov Rokowsky of Hadassa Hospital related that during Rav Aryeh Levine's illness, the latter expressed his concern over a pressing matter. "Oy, who knows if I have truly done enough praying for the welfare of others? When sick people come to me, asking that I pray for them, sometimes the words of Chazal creep into my mind: 'One who prays for his friend while he, too, is in need of the same salvation, will be answered first.'*
>
> *"Perhaps, deep down in my subconscious, I was really praying so I would recover from my illness first. Now I feel that I did not fulfill my mission to pray for them fervently enough. This is why I beg Hashem that He first answer the tefillos of those who come to me for help" (A Tzadik in Our Time).*

The Alter of Slobodka and Rav Chaim Shmulevitz knew the import of prayers on behalf of others.

One day the Alter was found standing in front of one of his student's house davening. When he was later asked why he chose to daven there, he explained that this student was having serious problems at home. The Alter had concluded that he was not davening adequately on his behalf because the yeshivah was too far removed from the student's sorrowful surroundings. The only way to truly relate to his struggles was by standing at the portals of his anguish. Once there it was possible to reach deep in his soul and sincerely daven on the student's behalf.

When Rav Chaim Shmulevitz was hospitalized with the illness that took his life, he discovered that a Torah scholar in another ward was critically ill. Rav Chaim asked to be taken to his room, despite the fact that every movement was painful for him. His family tried to dissuade him, but he insisted. When he was wheeled to the scholar's room, his fervent prayers were watered with his heartfelt tears (Siach Yisrael).

How to Get Your Prayers Answered

Preparing for Prayer

Entering *tefillah* mode requires devoting time to contemplating subjects that stir the heart and prepare it for prayer (*Sefer Ha'yirah*). At the very least, one should set aside a couple of moments of contemplation before starting to pray—just as one would prepare in advance for an important meeting (*Tefilas Channah*). The Kotzker Rebbe said that the time spent in sharpening the axe is as important as the time spent in chopping down the tree. *Tefillah* without preparation is not genuine *tefillah*: it ends up being exceedingly superficial (*R'Yechezkel Levenstein*).

Preparing for prayer is an ongoing commitment. A person who wants to maximize every encounter with Hashem must work to refine his character. An important pre-requisite to prayer is to reflect on our faults and resolve to change our ways. An individual who has not worked on self improvement and controlling his desires will never be able to pray with a clear mind, undistracted by alien, disturbing thoughts. A person with unequivocal faith will not be disrupted during his prayers (Rebbe Nachman of Breslov).

The Mashgiach of Kaminetz said, "It was my custom to come early to davening because I had heard that the sight of the Rebbe's [Rav Shraga Feivel Mendlowitz] preparation before davening was a remarkable spectacle. To see it was to witness greatness. I preceded him to the Bais Hamedrash and hid under the curtain.

"The Rebbe entered and thought no one was present. He began to recite korbanos. 'Le'olam yehay adam yerei shmayim baseser uvagoluy—Always let a person be G-d fearing privately and publicly... Ma anu ma chayenu ma chasdeinu—What are we? What is our life? What is our kindness?'

"He said this over and over, perhaps for fifteen minutes. He then continued, 'Halo kol hagiborim ki'ayin lifanecha ve'anshei hashem kelo hayu— Are not all the heroes like nothing before You? The famous as if they had never existed?'

"He repeated that, too, about ten or fifteen times. Then he continued, 'U'mosar ha'adam min ha'beheima oiyin—the pre-eminence of man over beast is non-existent,' saying it about ten or fifteen times.

"I was witnessing the Rebbe learning mussar. I tell you that at that moment my approach to tefillah was entirely transformed.

"Perhaps I was in error for not sharing what I saw with others, but I thought if it became public knowledge the Rebbe would begin his preparations at home, and I wanted to have the opportunity of observing him again and again."

"If I desire a burnt offering, I do not ask my angel Michael. From whom do I wish a sacrificial offering? From Yisrael" (*Midrash Tanchuma 96, 1*).

The Kotzker Rebbe wonders: how can a man's offering be preferable to an angel's? He explains that if Hashem seeks the action alone, then the angel Gavriel's deeds are purer than those of man. In fact, however, Hashem desires the intense preparation for the action, coupled with our resolution to overcome any obstacles, barriers, and distractions that may occur during prayer. In this realm, the angels cannot compete (*Lahavos Kodesh 52*).

When the granddaughter of Rabbi Schneur Zalman of Liadi married a grandson of Rabbi Levi Yitzchak of Berditchev, chassidim were given the opportunity to observe the routines of the two Rebbes who were now mechutonim.

At one point, Rabbi Schneur Zalman asked: "What's going on at the mechuton's?" The chassidim informed him that

Rabbi Levi Yitzchak had already finished with the morning prayers. "What a mechuton!" remarked the Rebbe. "He runs a hand over his eyes, and his soul is ready to soar in prayer. I could never manage such a feat—I cannot even begin to pray without several hours of preparation."

Later in the day, Rabbi Levi Yitzchak inquired after Rabbi Schneur Zalman and was told that the latter was still before his morning prayers. "What a mechuton!" said the Berditchever. "Whenever he arrives, he is accepted with open arms. As for myself, if I wish to enter the heavenly gates of prayer I must come at the appointed hour, when the door is open for all."

The Kotzker Rebbe advises us how to prepare for *tefillah*: "Before you *daven* in the morning, think to yourself, 'It would be nice to eat first. But I cannot do so because Hashem commands me not to, and I wish to act in accordance with His will. Why do I seek to fulfill His will? Because I fear the Holy One, Blessed Be He.'

"Then you should ask further, 'Why do I fear Hashem?' Your answer should be, 'Because He is the Creator of the entire universe, taking it from total nothingness into complex existence. Every single minute He watches over all the worlds and sustains them. But it is nevertheless within His power to nullify them all at any second. That is why I fear Him.'

"Finally, you should mentally long to be able to *daven* with devotion and fervor, and pray to grasp the magnitude of the Creator and the humbleness of your existence" (*Lahavos Kodesh 149*).

It is imperative to prepare our hearts for prayer—for we are mere dust and ashes, dependent upon the mercies of heaven for permission to enter the palace of the King.

The Midrash compares the results of primed prayer to a prince digging a tunnel to his father from the palace exterior, with the king digging toward him from within. Digging in Aramaic is called "Asira", which is one of the languages of prayer. In this type of prayer we approach Hashem after throwing ourselves into earnest groundwork, and Hashem responds in kind by hastening to meet up with us (Noam Siach).

The Slonimer Rebbe compared *davening* to planting. One first plows, then plants, then waters. Only then does the new growth begin to sprout. With *tefillah*, first we hollow out an opening in the heart, then we seed the words of prayer, and finally we pour out the tears of our hearts, so salvation will spring forth (*Bais Avraham*).

Despite great effort, the Belzer Rebbe Reb Aharon found it impossible to start his prayers on time. He was unable to begin until he felt personally qualified, and he therefore placed much stress on the mental preparations for prayer. Indeed, his preparations were extraordinary. He would donate substantial amounts of tzedaka with great concentration before proceeding (Rescuing the Rebbe of Belz).

The Kotzker Rebbe would expound on our sages' statement that one who says his prayers in a loud voice is considered a man with little faith. Surely one who avails himself of a method to arouse his *kavanah* should not be reviled as a man of limited faith! Yet he is classified as such, the Rebbe says, because he seeks ways of improving his devotion only *after* he began his prayers—not before (*Ha'osher She'betefillah*).

Rebbetzin Rivkah, one of the daughters-in-laws of the Tzemach Tzedek, once contracted a severe lung disease. A prominent specialist summoned from the capital despaired of her life. The Tzemach Tzedek calmed her. "The Talmud says that Torah has empowered doctors only to heal. Dire predictions are not in their province" (Berachos 60a).

He instructed his daughter-in-law to eat a breakfast of bread and butter immediately upon awakening, even before the morning prayers. "A Jew must be healthy, strong, and full of enthusiasm. The mitzvos must be permeated with spirited life." He also blessed her with long life.

Rebbetzin Rivkah felt her strength return as she followed the Rebbe's instructions. But she could not get over the distress at eating a hearty breakfast before her prayers. She decided to get up very early, so she could complete her prayers and then eat her breakfast at the time of day she would normally wake up. Now she felt she had the best of both worlds: though she ate breakfast early, she managed to pray beforehand.

When she related the details of her new schedule to the Tzemach Tzedek, he was displeased. "You have to be healthy," he said. "Better to eat in order to pray, than pray in order to eat" (HaYom Yom, 10 Shevat).

Rav Yechezkel Levenstein always arrived in shul early so he could properly prepare for his prayers. Only once did he come late to his prayers during the war years in Keidan. When he awoke that morning, he had discovered that a number of feathers had escaped his blanket and were scattered around the room. Because he was using the yeshivah's blanket he felt he was responsible for those feathers, and he was careful to collect them before leaving for the synagogue (Le'Shichno Tirdrishu).

Rav Levenstein paid a large sum to pay for cleaning help for a young married man, to enable him to arrive in shul early enough to prepare for his prayers. Rav Yechezkel knew that the young man invested great efforts in his davening; helping at home would deprive him of this preparation time (Ibid).

Do we not apply ourselves to our prayers because of pure laziness, or is it our tendency to give up too easily? It is difficult to determine. The Kotzker Rebbe would say that a person who invests no effort in his studies, readily forgives himself, and *davens* today because he davened yesterday, will be overcome by the forces of evil *(Ha'osher She'betefillah*).

If prayer is important to us, we will develop personal methods that are effective in arousing our feelings while *davening*. We must start out by acknowledging that without Hashem's help we would not succeed at prayer. We are limited; it is only appropriate that we ask for Divine assistance to pray properly. If we turn to Hashem for help, He will certainly respond.

The Kedushas Levy explains the superfluous word "saying" in the verse "I implored Hashem at that time, saying" (*Devarim 3, 23*), as a reference to prayer before prayer. Moshe Rabenu implored Hashem that he should properly speak his words of prayer (*Avir Yaakov, 11 Elul*).

The verse in *Tehillim* (*118, 25*), "*Ana Hashem hoshiah na*," is generally translated as, "I pray to You, Hashem, please help me." R' Boruch of Mezhibozh explained it as, "Please, Hashem, help me pray to You," for the word "na" is a language of prayerful request.

An alarmingly understaffed hospital had only one doctor on call, when there should have been at least four doctors available to handle the various emergencies, which were a common occurrence in the intensive care unit.

Perhaps during a quiet evening one doctor might have been adequate—but this was never the case. The patients had to be tended to, their equipment painstakingly monitored, their infusions precisely adjusted. Under the best of conditions, the solitary doctor was dashing from one bed to another all evening.

One evening soon after the beginning of the night shift, one of the patients awoke and began screaming loudly, waking everyone in the ward. Havoc reigned as each patient demanded assistance. The doctor was so busy responding to the cries that he neglected to check on the one silent patient hooked up to the heart monitor. When he eventually remembered to check his monitor, no adjustments were needed—the patient was no longer among the living.

Charges were pressed against the doctor. The judge reprimanded him for his negligence. The doctor tried to justify his neglect, explaining that he just couldn't manage alone. But the judge would not accept that excuse: "Why didn't you call for help?" he demanded.

Very often a person will begin his *Amidah* prayer with wonderful intentions. He plans to *daven* on behalf a relative who isn't well in the blessing "*Refaeinu*". He wants to have his newly married son in mind during the blessing "*Bureich*

Aleinu". He wishes to mention various other personal issues in "*Selach Lanu*".

Then he starts to *daven*, and he suddenly finds himself at the blessing "*Teka B'Shofar*". He asks himself, "How did I get here?" This awful scenario may repeat itself at *Mincha* and *Maariv*.

Instead of beginning to focus as we say the words "*Baruch Atah*" of the blessing "*Magen Avraham*", we should focus on the request that we say just prior to the *Amidah* prayers: "*Yeheyu l'razton imrei pi*". We must beg Hashem to open our mouths and help us *daven*. Without this *tefillah* we will never succeed (*Sheifos pp. 223-224*). We should then mentally express our resolve to *daven* with self-sacrifice, with all our energy and concentration.

Do Not Delay Your Prayers

Our prayers have little value if we pursue other ways to find relief, turning to Hashem only after all else has failed. If you want your prayers answered, you must pray first!

It is best to avoid conversation before prayer in the morning. It is exceedingly difficult to go from a casual conversation with a friend to a profound conversation with Hashem. A person who studies Torah before praying purifies his mind, so his senses are readied for prayer. Since it is far easier to concentrate with a pure mind, it is a good idea to learn before *davening* (*Meor*

Ve'Shemesh Bereishis).

If prayer is not at the top of our list of priorities, our prayers will not readily receive Hashem's attention. Reflect on the fact that all other efforts are meaningless unless they are powered by our *tefillos*.

> *Our sages inform us that it was decreed numerous times that Moshe would not enter the Land of Israel—but the decree was not finalized. Although Moshe was told that he would not be crossing the Jordan River, his reaction was tempered by his knowledge that every time the Jewish people had sinned grievously, he had been able to attain forgiveness for them through his prayers. He did not feel the need to pray immediately; he was confident that, since he had never sinned, Hashem would respond positively to his prayers (Devarim Rabbah 11, 10 see commentaries ad loc). Because Moshe Rabeinu postponed his appeal, the original decree was ultimately reinforced by Hashem's non-rescindable oath. Rav Eliyahu Lopian remarks that this Midrash teaches us the importance of reacting immediately to any grave pronouncement by hastening to pray. This insures that our prayers will not remain unanswered (Lev Eliyahu, Shevivei Lev 185).*

When a distressing event occurs, our first reaction should be to pray. Rebbe Nosson often cited the well-known dictum, "*Ein rega bli pega*," which is usually translated as, "there is no moment without difficulties." An alternate translation of *pega* is request. Rebbe Nosson suggests that there should not to be a moment without prayerful requests. If we are constantly making requests of Hashem, we will be saved from all difficulties.

Rabbi Hillel of Paritch was once struck with an immense longing to spend Shabbos with his Rebbe, Rabbi Menachem Mendel of Lubavitch. Getting there was another matter, as it was already late in the week and many miles separated Babroisk from Lubavitch.

A young chassid offered to take him; with his sleek coach and superb horses, they would be able to make it in time. But because time was short, Rabbi Hillel had to agree to two conditions. They would take the highway—which Rabbi Hillel normally did not use, since it had been constructed by the wicked Czar Nikolai—and Rabbi Hillel would keep his prayers short. Having no other option, Rabbi Hillel agreed.

That night they slept at a wayside inn. In the morning the young fellow prayed and breakfasted, then looked in on Rabbi Hillel who was still praying. A short time later he checked on him again. He was in the same position. Hours went by, and still the older chassid continued to pour out his heart before his Creator.

When Rabbi Hillel finally finished, his companion was quite upset. "I don't understand," he complained. "You wanted to spend Shabbos with the Rebbe, and you promised to hurry with your prayers. Now there is no chance of reaching Lubavitch on time!"

Answered Reb Hillel, "Suppose you wished to journey to the Leipzig fair to purchase some rare merchandise, available nowhere else. But on the way you met another merchant offering the same wares at a good price. Only a fool would say, 'But I must go to Leipzig!' The purpose is not the town, but the merchandise.

"I travel to the Rebbe to seek guidance on praying with love and awe of G-d. If my praying goes well on the way to Lubavitch, should I dump the merchandise and run to Leipzig?"

Hashem Awaits Our Prayers

The early Chassidim "*Hayu shohim*—would tarry" for an hour prior to their prayers to direct their hearts to Hashem (*Berachos 30*). An alternate explanation for "*shohim"* is to wonder. They would spend the hour in wonderment at Hashem's greatness (*Noam Elimelech*). Hashem is our Father in Heaven. He loves us unconditionally, without any limitations. There is nothing He does not want to give us, and there is nothing He cannot give us, for the entire world is His.

In *Shir Hashirim* (2:14), Hashem addresses the Jewish people. "Show me your prayerful gaze; let Me hear your supplicating voice, for your voice is sweet and your countenance comely."

This verse is a reference to Hashem's desire to hear His children's prayer. The verse "*Ve'atah kadosh yoshev tehilos Yisrael*" (*Tehillim 22:4*) is interpreted as a reference to Hashem sitting and waiting for the praises of the Jewish people (*Rashi*).

Hashem wants us to keep praying. "I am your G-d Who hoisted you out of Egypt; open wide your mouth, and I will fill it." (*Tehillim* 81). Hashem wants us to fill our mouths with prayer; in turn, He promises to respond by filling our mouths with good (*Sichos Mussar 28*).

Even those who have not properly honed their ability to pray may turn to Hashem in times of need—for He is a loving Father. He is always waiting and receptive to revitalizing our contact with Him, just as any parent would be whose child had broken off their relationship.

Rabbi Y. Y. Rubinstein of England demonstrates this with a very touching story that he often relates in his lectures:

> *A few years ago I was concluding a talk in front of a very large audience in London. After I had finished and everyone had left, one man remained behind. He approached and asked me if I lived in Manchester, and I confirmed that I did. He inquired which area in Manchester, and I told him. His next question was whether I knew a certain person who lived there, and I answered yes.*
>
> *"How is he getting on?" he asked. The man continued*

with a whole series of questions about this person. "What does he do for a living? How many children does he have and how old are they?"

I tried my best to answer, but since I didn't know the person very well, I couldn't be sure about some details.

Then it was my turn to pose a question. "How do you know him?" I asked.

My questioner looked at me intensely, and a very sad and pensive expression passed across his face. He hesitated, looked down at the floor, and very quietly replied, "He's my son."

I was taken aback. After a moment I asked, "How is it that you don't know how many grandchildren you have?"

I listened to his tale of a rebellious teenage son who had gone off the deep end in a big way. The parents had tried every device they could think of to make their son see sense. They had tried bribery and threats, and had gotten other people to talk to him, but nothing had worked.

One night, in both frustration and desperation, the father had screamed at his son, "Get out! Get out and never come back!"

And that's exactly what the boy did. Fifteen years later the son had settled down and built his own family, but he had never come back or had any contact with his parents.

I listened with great sadness. I told the father that although I didn't know his son well, I felt sure he would like to see his father again. The father shook his head firmly. "It`s too late now. Too much water has flowed under the bridge."

Then an idea struck me. I suggested that if he gave me his address and phone number, I could send him regular reports on how his son and his family were getting along. The father liked this idea, and so we parted with me promising to keep in touch.

When I returned to Manchester, by coincidence I bumped into his son. (You can always arrange coincidences!) I told him I had just returned from London and had met someone there who was asking after him. He inquired who it was. I paused and said, "Your father."

He looked at me for a moment and then asked, "How is he getting on?"

It was obvious that the son was as concerned for the father as the father was for the son. I told him that I thought his father wanted to see him, and—uncannily—he replied in the identical manner as his father had. "I don't think so. Too much water has flowed under the bridge."

I tried to persuade him he was wrong. Then I tried a

different approach. "By coincidence I am going back down to London in three days. Suppose I were to take you to see your father?"

The son hesitated, but I was able to convince him to agree.

When I arrived home, I phoned the father and asked him if he would be at home on that Thursday at one o'clock. He probably assumed I intended to phone with a report, and confirmed that he would be in. I told him that I was bringing his son to see him, and before he could reply I said goodbye and hung up.

The drive to London passed unusually quickly. We located the house right away, and I walked up to the door with my very nervous companion.

A very long time seemed to elapse before the door opened. The man who had had so many questions a few days before stood anxiously, looking at the face of the son he had not seen for fifteen years. I watched as tears welled up in his eyes and started to course down his cheeks. I looked at the son, and he, too, had tear-filled eyes. The son took one step toward his father, and the father rushed toward his son, and they folded each other in a hug. After a few moments they turned and walked into the house. I found myself wonderfully redundant, and paused to wipe the tears from my own cheeks before getting into my car for the drive back to Manchester.

A few months later the son bought a house in London, and moved there with his family to be near his father.

This is the relationship Hashem has with us. He is our Father, as the verse states, "You are the children of Hashem" (*Devarim 14:1*). No matter how much a child has wronged his parents, as long as he sincerely regrets what he has done, they will always take him back.

Hashem Wants to Help Us

When we *daven* we should *expect* Hashem to answer our prayers. We are the children of the Creator of the Universe; we can be certain that the Creator will come through for us. We should never become discouraged, even if it appears that our prayers are being ignored. Perhaps we are lacking just one more prayer to make up the total that will set our salvation in motion. Because it is so easy to lose heart, the verse prods us to remain hopeful and enthusiastic: "Trust in Hashem, strengthen your hearts, and trust in Hashem" (Tehillim 27).

When a river is dammed, the flow of water is held back from its natural course. Removing the dam causes the water to gush forth in torrents, returning to its natural course. More than anything else, Hashem wants to help us. We need to simply remove the obstacles that prevent Hashem from assisting us. Then—either through natural means, or miraculous means—Hashem will come through for us ... as long as we *believe* it.

We must put ourselves in Hashem's hands. The natural by-product of that trust is a special intimacy, which enables us to interact with Hashem without any walls holding back His miracles.

When Rav Yehudah Kerwitz, a student of the Chofetz Chaim, would see a young boy begging for something from his father he would remark, "This is exactly how the Chofetz Chaim davened." In Shema Koleinu he would speak to Hashem in Yiddish, as a child speaks to his father, making requests for himself and the Jewish people (Meir Einei Yisrael Part one page 234).

When a downtrodden Jew came to the Chofetz Chaim complaining of his miserable situation, the Chofetz Chaim told him, "I was orphaned when I was young. Whenever I needed something, I would take my Tehillim, stand in a corner, and pray. Hashem would always hear my prayers and help me. Do the same, and Hashem will surely help you."

The Chofetz Chaim could not understand why people would line up to get a blessing from him. "Why do you think you need my help with our Father? A father is not pleased when one of his children asks for something on behalf of another child. He wants each child to approach him directly. It is the same with our Father in Heaven. Hashem wants us each to turn to him with our own requests.

"If you transgressed, and think your Father might be angry, I reassure you that He greatly desires you to make up with Him. He waits for you to approach him. You must first daven yourself!"

One of the Kotzker Rebbe's followers came to him with a request. "Rebbe, please pray for me. I need heavenly mercy!"

The Rebbe fixed his eyes on him in admonishment. "Are you too ill to wrap yourself in your tallis and daven for yourself?" (Lahavos Kodesh 131)

Focus on Your Prayers

A one-year-old opens a *siddur* and intently shakes back and forth. His parents watch with smiles of delight as their precocious young son appears to be praying. But when he is eight or nine, simply swaying back and forth is not enough. His parents expect him to say the words properly, and if he cannot read without mistakes, they are deeply distressed.

When one's heart and mind are not meditating in unison, he is praying like the toddler. A knowledgeable person is expected to pray with greater intensity. We need to plow, seed and nourish our prayers with the maturity and wisdom that Hashem has granted us (*Introduction to Tefilas Channah p. 43*).

Prayer is referred to as a labor. What exertion is required of us? The Ramban explains that a man's thoughts are all over the place. In a short time he can think about hundreds of things. As we pray, various thoughts vie for our attention—thoughts which have nothing to do with prayer. The effort to halt this stream of thoughts and focus on our prayer is the exertion required of us … and it is not easy (*Ramban, Shir Ha'Shirim*).

Nullify foreign thoughts by saying to yourself, "Hashem, I want to think only of the words of *tefillah* and only of you. Help me nullify any foreign thought that enter my mind while I am *davening* for I do not want any part of them at all."

> *Rav Shlomo Zalman Auerbach was once asked what resolutions he made for Rosh Hashana. He replied, "To recite the first blessing of Shemoneh Esrei with kavannah" (The Man of Truth and Peace, p. 127).*

When a person *davens*, he should be oblivious to his environment; all his senses should be focused on the words of prayer. The Steipler defined *kavanah* as saying the words aloud, so we can hear and reflect on that which we have said (*LeShichno Tidrishu*).

This is the meaning of "calling out to Hashem in truth". How focused should he be? Like a person listening to a fascinating story, who doesn't want to miss a single detail. He is oblivious to that which is happening around him—all his senses are directed toward the storyteller. He hears no noise, feels no hunger, thirst, cold, tiredness or pain.

Reb Aharon of Kremenchung was once davening at home when a fire broke out. Everyone in the house began to scream, along with some neighbors who had come to the rescue. Reb Aharon remained locked in his room and heard nothing. In the end they had to break down the door. When they entered they discovered that he was still sitting and davening. They carried him out through the window, but he still remained completely oblivious to what was happening to him. When he finally finished his prayers he asked, "Where am I? What happened?" (Diary of Rav Yosef Yitzchak Schneersohn)

We must make every effort not to let thoughts of worldly concern enter our minds, so our prayers remain pure (*Reb Nochum of Tchernobel, Hanhagos Tzaddikim p. 35*).

The Belzer Rebbe, Reb Aharon's prayers were clearly enunciated with fear, awe, and usually with speed. Occasionally he was so consumed by a fiery passion that he would roar whole sentences and paragraphs in one breath. On other, rarer occasions, his fervent prayers would stretch for protracted periods. At those times all that could be heard were intermittent groans and sighs, but his coloring would change rapidly. Sometimes clouds of worry would cross his face; later, his countenance would glow with an ethereal light. When he began to pray, his physical frailties seemed to disappear. He was invigorated by the service of Hashem, his face aflame with an inner fire, his prayers animated with warmth and spirit (Rescuing the Rebbe of Belz).

The Rambam cites two contradictory *halachos* related to concentrating during the *Amidah* prayer. In chapter four of the Laws of Prayer, he writes that if one says *Shemoneh Esrei* without *kavanah*, he has not fulfilled his obligation. In chapter ten he writes that if one focuses on the first blessing, he has fulfilled his obligation for the *Shemoneh Esrei* prayer.

Rav Chaim Soloveitchik resolves the contradiction by distinguishing between two types of *kavanah*. The first category, is knowing the meaning of the words. The second is being conscious of standing before Hashem while praying. The first type of *kavanah* suffices for the first blessing, while the second is required for the rest of the *Amidah* prayer. A person who does not visualize himself as communicating with Hashem is simply moving his mouth to no purpose (*Ha'osher Sheb'tefillah*). A good technique is to imagine being surrounded by Hashem's light. At the same time remind yourself that Hashem is listening to you as you speak.

Reb Dov Ber of Mezritch explains why so many foreign thoughts interfere during davening, making it nearly impossible to avoid them without siyata di'shmaya. In fact, sometimes, the harder one tries to daven, the more distracting thoughts he entertains. He explains this with a parable.

If a man has a bright son who learns well, giving him much nachas, he will take advantage of this source of pleasure by having every learned guest test his son. The harder and more confusing the questions, the more pleased the father will be—as long as his son knows the answers. A good guest will go to great lengths to try to stump the son to please his host.

In the same vein, the harder one tries to daven, the harder the Yetzer Hara tries to distract him. If he is able to overcome the evil inclination and continue davening fervently—how pleased Hashem will be! (Yosher Divrei Emes p.22)

A person should interrupt himself again and again, if necessary, strengthening and arousing a burning, pure love and fear of Hashem. One should say to oneself, "Hashem, I love you," or alternately, "Hashem I believe in you." Then all prayers will soar aloft, bringing joy and pleasure to his Maker (*Seder Chaim of Rabbi Shalom Schachna of Probitsch; Dvir Yaakov, p. 8*).

Rav Yosef Dayan was once hospitalized. A visitor found Rav Yosef connected to an intravenous drip and sundry monitors, standing at his bedside praying Mincha. The man stood in the doorway, patiently waiting for Rav Yosef to complete his prayers. He assumed that, given Rav Yosef's condition, the Amidah would soon be over. After waiting for forty minutes, the healthy visitor began to find it difficult to keep standing. He was astounded that the Rav was still going strong. When Rav Yosef finally took three steps back at the end of his prayer, he collapsed on his bed, completely drained from his efforts (Od Yosef Chai page 144).

Making Changes

Sometimes commitments are required to invest our prayers with additional clout. They range from assuming additional obligations to dramatic lifestyle changes.

When a yeshivah student became afflicted with a dreaded disease, doctors operated but soon despaired of his life. The boy's father came to the Manchester Rosh Yeshivah, who told him that if he dedicated his son's life to Torah, he would have a full recovery. The father had been planning for his son to embark on a career; now he readily agreed to the Rosh Yeshivah's proposal. That night, as the Rosh Yeshivah whispered the Shemoneh Esrei of Maariv, he was heard saying, "Tate, ich hob em tzugezogt—Father, I promised him." Later, he told another student, "I am telling you, he will be healthy once again."

Shortly afterward the parents placed their son under the care of another doctor, who determined that the patient's alarming weakness was the result of his having been given the wrong medication. A new medication was prescribed. To everyone's amazement, the boy was soon strong enough to undergo a second operation. Today he is a healthy, outstanding Torah scholar who has raised a beautiful family.

With Joy

Joy is the preferred method of prayer (Rav Bunim of Peshischa). When a person's joy extends down to his fingertips, expressing itself in spontaneous clapping of the hands, Esav's hands are disabled so that his descendants are powerless to harm us (Rav Yaakov Yosef of Polnoa). The *sefer Chassidim* notes that the root of prayer is joy in Hashem, as the verse states, "Praise His holy Name, the heart of those who seek Hashem shall rejoice" (*Divrei Ha'Yamim I, 16:10*). When a person truly senses that he is addressing the One Who has the solution to all his problems, he rises to his feet with enthusiasm, joyful for this opportunity he has been given (*Shearim Be'tefillah p. 49*).

Prayer—and especially *Pesukei Dezimrah*—should be said slowly, with a pleasant, strong voice, as the verse (*Ezra 3:12*) states, "To raise my voice in joy." One of the functions of *Pesukei Dezimrah* is to infuse our prayers with joy (*Tosfos 31a and Rosh Berachos 5,2*).

> *A poor man who presents himself to the king while weeping copiously and loudly, bemoaning his difficult circumstances, will receive a small donation—then will quickly be constrained to leave. A poor man who uses his audience to joyfully praise the king, while adding a request for funds, will have his request generously fulfilled*

(Ha'Mayan Ha'nitzchi).

A person should pray in whichever synagogue his heart desires, in the same way that he is advised to study the subject matter he is fond of (*Avoda Zara 19*). Why is this important? Praying in a relaxed environment in pleasant company revitalizes the spirit and fills the heart with joy (*Responsa of the Ridvaz*).

With Tears

Rav Yonoson Eibeshitz observed that the numerical value of *bechi,* weeping, is 32—identical to that of *lev,* heart. Tears are only meaningful if they are sincere expressions of the heart (*Yaaros Devash*).

Tefillah at its best is accompanied by tears. Not tears of sadness or anger but tears of *hachnaah,* humility. Tears of total submission break through the barriers that exist between Hashem and us. These tears go straight through the Gates of Tears to heaven.

The Chassam Sofer had three taleisim. They were cleaned monthly in rotation to remove the grime, which accumulated as a result of the copious tears he shed when he prayed (Olamo Shel Aba page 67).

Since the destruction of the Bais Hamikdash, the gates of

tefillah are often blocked by our sins. The only force capable of shattering these barriers is the tears accompanying prayer, which indicate that a person has cast off his own presumptuous ego, allowing his genuine feelings of devotion to surface. This characterizes total dedication.

A distraught woman who had been recently widowed came to Rav Aryeh Levine for consolation. All his efforts to raise her spirits were to no avail. "What happened to all of my tears?" she asked. "I prayed countless prayers, said chapters of Tehillim without number, and shed tears constantly. My very soul flowed into those tears. Were they all wasted?"

Gently, Rav Aryeh replied, "After a hundred and twenty years you will see how meaningful and precious your tears were. You will discover that Hashem gathered and counted every single teardrop. Each droplet is cherished like a priceless gem. When a harsh and evil decree loomed over the Jewish people, one of your tears came and washed the evil away, making it null and void. A simple, sincere tear is a cause of salvation!"

The woman burst into a fresh flow of tears. Not tears of sorrow and grief, this time, but tears of courage and hopefulness (Overview of Art Scroll Kinos).

The mother of the Kol Aryeh would go to shul to listen to the lectures of Rav Amram Chasida, the local rav. Even in the ninth month of her pregnancy she insisted on attending the rav's sermon, slowly making her way to the women's section of the shul.

In middle of the lecture, sobbing was heard from her location. Family members rushed to her side, concerned that she was about to give birth. They were surprised to find her sitting calmly, though crying with great emotion. "I was praying for Hashem to grant me a son who will be able to inspire people like our rav," she explained.

Later that night she gave birth to a son who became one of the greatest rabbis in Hungary (Aleinu Le'Shabeach Vayikra pg. 219).

Reitzah Golda, the mother of R' Yehoshua Tzvi Michel Shapira, fasted regularly and prayed to merit a worthy son. She went from one gravesite to another, often while fasting, beseeching Hashem to grant her request.

Hashem blessed her with a son who was a great tzaddik. The young Tzvi Michel forged his own path to holiness by studying the behavior of many great, righteous individuals in the heavenly city of Yerushalayim. Every Shabbos he joined the minyan of Rav Shimon Menashe so he could observe him at his prayers.

Throughout his life he cried profusely during his prayers, stopping only when his eyesight was at risk. "How can a person expect to get close to Hashem," he would say, "if he does not permit the tears to gush from his heart at least half an hour each day?" (Tzvi Le'Zaddik)

The municipal government announced that it would begin to tax renters. A young man came to Rav Silberstein in tears. His rent would now be raised from five hundred to seven hundred dollars monthly, and he had no way of paying the additional money.

The Rav did his best to reassure the young man, and encouraged him to continue praying. Soon afterward, the tax was annulled.

In retelling the story Rav Silberstein would remark, "No doubt the prayers and tears of the young man and others like him were responsible for the government's change of heart" (Tuvcha Yabiu I, p. 135).

An American Jew with nine children endured the anguish of seeing one child after another leave Yiddishkeit. Only the youngest remained at home. The father desperately tried to convince him to attend a yeshiva. But the son wished to be like his brothers, sisters and friends, and he told his father that he wasn't interested in remaining observant.

His father begged him not to go the way of his siblings. "You are my last hope!" he told his son, as bitter tears flowed down his cheeks. But the son would only promise that he would try to remain religious. It wasn't long before his promises were forgotten, and the son joined the ranks of assimilated American Jewry.

Year passed. The son, now a grown man, had a son of his own who was named after his father. The young man wrote to his father, telling him that he was studying at Yeshiva Ohr Somayach so he could learn what it means to be a Jew. The father flew to Israel, ready to talk his son out of his foolishness.

Then he remembered his own father's tears.

Those tears succeeded in bringing back both father and son to Torah-true Yiddishkeit. On the anniversary of the father's yahrzeit, his son celebrated a siyum mishnayos (Jewish Observer Dec. 98, p.47).

With All Your Heart

A *tefillah* is rated, not by the intensity of the mouth's cry, but by the intensity of the heart (*Rav Yechezkel Levenstein, Mofes Hador p. 136*).

The Kohen Gadol had to pray for Hashem to send the rains the crops needed, and to ignore the prayers of those who were on the road and did not want to get caught in the rain. The traveler always davens from the bottom of his heart, for he knows that only Hashem can help him. This heartfelt prayer slices through the heavens to Hashem's Throne of Glory, and could only be counteracted by the prayer of the Kohen Gadol (Alter of Kelm on Yoma 53).

The same concept applies to the prayers of those exiled to the cities of refuge. The mother of the Kohen Gadol would care for these unfortunates so they not pray for the demise of her son—since the death of the Kohen Gadol would set them free. Why did she have to worry so about the prayers of those who had extinguished the life of another? Clearly their heartfelt prayers were significant enough to make an impression Above. Even unworthy prayers that are uttered with great emotion have an immense effect.

A young Torah scholar told Rav Silberstein his mother's poignant story: "I was born after ten years of childlessness. My mother's years of anguish were transformed to great joy at my birth. She couldn't thank Hashem enough, and was determined to help others who had not yet been blessed with a child. She resolved to pray on their behalf.

"My mother was walking down the street one day when she noticed a lady who appeared deeply distressed. She asked what was troubling her. It turned out that although she had been married sixteen years, the woman had no children.

"My mother asked for her name and her mother's name. She then warmly blessed the woman that Hashem should remember her quickly.

"Nine months later to the day, the woman called to tell her that she had just had a boy."

The young man added, "My mother puts her heart and soul into her prayers for those who are childless. We know of four other children born as a result of her tefilos" (Aleinu Le'Shabeach Vayikra p. 212).

Rav Moshe Midner alerted his followers to the multi-faceted tactics of the *yetzer hara*. The evil inclination adjusts his strategies regularly to seduce us into sin. For a material transgression he stirs up our enthusiasm, heating it to a fervent pitch. When we are involved in spiritual activities, such as Torah study and *davening*, he turns down the thermostat, causing us to become frozen and dispassionate. Our task is to summon enthusiasm and excitement for our prayers, fully engaging our hearts.

We repeat many of our prayers approximately 1,100 times during the year. This repetition can result in mindless recitation of the words. It is up to us to make an effort to regenerate enthusiasm for our prayers. Studying various commentaries on the *siddur* can help. On occasion, simply closing our eyes and praying by heart can enable us to summon moving thoughts to enhance our prayers. One suggestion, by Rav Yerucham Levovitz, is to consider changing one's regular place to a more inspiring milieu to regenerate enthusiasm.

Rav S. Pincus noted that prayer is a weapon which is not tied to our merits—only to the earnestness of our plea. King Chizkiyahu turned his face to the wall and prayed to Hashem to give him more years of life. The Gemara informs us (*Berachos* 10) that Reish Lakish defines "turning his face to the wall" as turning inward to the walls of his heart—praying from the depths of his heart. When our hearts are not involved in our prayers, our mouths are transformed into an express train which brings us to the end of *shemoneh esrei*—before we manage to formulate our requests.

How do we rouse our hearts? We must go beyond intellectual comprehension of the words and begin to feel their meaning. When we ask for forgiveness for our sins, we must feel the heartbreak of having created a barrier between ourselves and our Father in Heaven. When we ask for compassion on Tzion, we must feel that life is not worth living without the Bais Hamikdash (*Ohel Miriam p. 133*).

How do we achieve this level of emotion? The following parable will help us acquire the proper techniques:

There was a destitute man, never far from starvation, who spent months assuaging his hunger with dreams of the approaching wedding of the son of the richest man in town. The father of the chassan would always send a special wagon to collect the poor of the city and set before them a feast fit for a king.

Our poor hero ate nothing the day of the wedding to ensure that he had a good appetite for the wedding feast. When he got really hungry, he ate just a morsel of bread and a bit of water. He wanted to have enough room for all the good food he would be served that night.

By the time the sun set he was ravenous. He sat waiting for the wagon that would take him to the festivities—but it failed to arrive! His hunger pangs threatened to overwhelm him. He saw no wagon on the horizon. The sky was very dark; the wedding feast had certainly begun, yet no one had come to get him. The poor man finally concluded that there was no point waiting. He reached into his basket and found a piece of dry black bread with two small onions, which he ate with tears coursing down his cheeks. He would not enjoy the wedding feast he had been dreaming of for so long.

The man hadn't eaten all day, and his usual supper had left him hungry. He dug deep into his basket and unearthed another chunk of bread, which he ate with another two onions he discovered in the pantry. Finally he was full.

Just as he had completed his meal, a knock came at the door. Totally out of breath, the visitor announced that the wagon was waiting outside to take the poor man to the wedding.

Our hero was heartbroken. What was the point in going? He wouldn't be able to eat anything! The rich man's messenger urged him not to be foolish, and to get into the cart. In the end, the poor man could not resist.

In a short time he found himself seated at the banquet hall. He saw all his friends eating with great appetite, their eyes shinning with joy. He tried tasting the tantalizing dishes that were being served, one after another. It was too difficult to resist. Ignoring the complaints of his overworked stomach, he proceeded to do full justice to the meal set before him.

The poor man could have gone on like that indefinitely—but then disaster struck. Suddenly his stomach heaved, and he began vomiting everything he had eaten. His stomach was left completely empty.

We feel compassion for the unfortunate man who was reduced to eating dried bread with onions when he had an elaborate feast waiting for him. In fact, we can be compared to this poor man. Our hearts are full of the spiritual equivalent of black bread and onions—jealousy, lust, and desire for honor. There is absolutely no room for a serving of spirituality; no place for prayers and praises. It is impossible to cry with sincerity when our hearts are engaged elsewhere.

Without heart, there are no tears—and without heart, there is no prayer. The world is full of permissiveness and confusion. When we allow these concerns to enter our hearts, pure emotions are dulled, and the innate passion for all things holy evaporates. It is no wonder that even a crumb of spirituality cannot enter.

We await the fulfillment of the prophecy that hearts of flesh will replace our hearts of stone. Only a heart free of desire for materialism and empty of the need for luxuries can become a font of wholesome tears.

How can we initiate the process of converting our hearts to hearts of flesh? We must begin by cultivating our hearts' positive aspects: all negative desires must be pushed aside. The study of Torah mellows the heart. We must focus on flashes of inspiration, taking advantage of all possible spiritual input in the form of Torah lectures. When the heart softens, love and fear will enter (*Kotzker vort*).

> *A young Torah scholar who devoted himself to Torah study and the service of Hashem began experiencing serious personal problems. He was having problems with his children, his shalom bayis had deteriorated, parnassa was almost nil… the list seemed to be without end.*
>
> *He went to one of the leaders of our generation to pour out*

his broken heart. The Rav heard him out and asked, "Have you davened?"

"Of course!" he replied.

The Rav was not satisfied. "Have you prayed as you ought? Have you prayed with deep-seated confidence that Hashem can help you?"

The young scholar said nothing. He realized that though he had repeatedly prayed for salvation, he was never fired with conviction that only Hashem could ameliorate his situation.

He left the Rav's study and went to daven. His prayers were uttered with sincerity and warmth. After several prayers of ardent faith, he found that almost all his problems were resolved (Sheifos pp. 215-216).

A young boy in Ramat Sharon, one of the best students in the Talmud Torah of Ramat Elchanan, fell from a tall building and was seriously injured. The child was rushed to the hospital in critical condition. The doctors did not believe he would survive.

The principal of the school was desperate to do something for the youngster. He ran to catch the 400 bus to the Kosel, so he could pray there for the recovery of his student.

When he arrived at the Kosel there were a group of yeshiva boys praying with great devotion. At 5:45 the principal began praying with intense concentration. When he reached the blessing of "Refaeinu" he began to weep, imploring Hashem to heal the child. As he finished the blessing, the group of boys burst into song.

The principal completed his prayers and returned to Ramat Elchanan. When he got home he discovered that at the exact moment he had said the blessing "Refaeinu," the child came out of the coma and asked for a drink of water. A few days later he was back in school, completely recovered (Tuvcha Yabiu II, p. 282).

If we rouse ourselves to pray with all our hearts, we, too, will witness miracles.

External Strategies

Sometimes it is necessary to wake our physical bodies with sound and movements when we begin to pray, to allow the power of the soul to shine through. The Zohar teaches, "If the fire does not burn intensely, tap the wood, and it blazes forth. To the same effect, if the light of the soul does not burn brightly, tap the body, so the light of the soul will blaze forth" (*Zohar 3:168a*).

When Rabbi Mordechai of Lechovitz prayed, he roared like a lion until the hearts of all who heard him would shatter and melt like water (Mazkeret Shem ha'Gedolim).

The rebbe Reb Elimelech recommended, "Pray with all your strength. Use your voice to arouse your feelings, and connect your thoughts to your words. Face the wall, look into the *siddur* morning and evening, and do not look to the side from the commencement of the service until the end. When the reader repeats the *Amidah*, follow along inside the *siddur* and answer *amen* to each blessing with all your strength" (*Tzetel Katan 11*).

When a person succeeds in lighting up his soul, the body becomes less and less significant—until he prays with the soul alone. One who does this successfully can worship in thought, without any motion (*Likutei Yekarim 33*).

Pray Again and Again

When you succeed at praying in an uplifting fashion, do not conclude that you have done your duty. There are some illnesses that require ten days of antibiotics, while others may require a daily dose of medication. You must follow the prescribed regimen carefully to achieve results.

Prayer works the same way. The problem is, we are not told exactly how long it will take. We dare not reduce the measure of the prayer treatment. Pray, and do not despair, for despair is the tool of the evil inclination. The Midrash reassures us that whoever prays often will be answered (*Yalkut Shmuel 1, 78*).

When the Jewish people were threatened by their Arab neighbors the Belzer Rebbe Reb Aharon prayed at great length. Friday night, when arriving for Kabbolas Shabbos, he paused at the mezuzah of his room for a significant period, silently praying with fervor. He then approached the Shabbos candles and stood there for three solid hours, davening without respite. Friday night davening did not begin until midnight and lasted until twenty minutes before daybreak.

The lengthy prayer continued all week through the next Shabbos, and then the week after. At eleven o'clock on Shabbos morning, the third week of the war which was essentially over, the door of his room was opened as usual so the Rav could hear the Torah leining. When the ba'al koreh reached the words, "Ve'Yaakov halach ledarko, Jacob went on his way," the Rebbe told them to pause while he again began praying.

Eventually the chassidim continued the leining and completed mussaf, while the Rebbe remained engrossed in fervent prayer through that Shabbos and beyond nightfall. He continued until long after midnight, completing his prayer at 3:55 in the morning—praying for over sixteen hours. This, at a time when he was so weak that he could barely stand without assistance (Rescuing the Rebbe of Belz).

When a person senses that Hashem is not listening, he should remind himself that Hashem is putting him to the test to see if he can rise above despair and stay focused. If he is not distracted and continues to pray with confidence, his deliverance may be at hand. It may sometimes appear that the situation has worsened with increased prayer. Hashem is concealing Himself to see if we will seek Him out, or simply give up. By renewing his prayer a person demonstrates that he is still committed to the quest for salvation. When he falters, he should pray to Hashem to help him keep praying.

Even if one sees no visible results, he should continue praying, for the ripple effects of prayer are considerable. Noach made the mistake of not praying for his generation because he believed his prayers would not help a generation steeped in sin. The Zohar suggests that had he prayed, he could have saved them (*See Pnei Menachem Noach 1992*). The Imrei Emes points out that a Jew must always pray, whether his prayers are answered or not.

It is a terrible mistake to conclude that one's prayers have accomplished nothing. Each and every word of prayer is genuinely valuable. Prayer is our obligation, and it brings pleasure to Hashem.

Avraham should be the prototype of prayer under all circumstances. He did not stop praying for Sodom's salvation, even after the angels left to destroy the city (*Hischazkus Be'tefillah La'Hashem*).

"The person who is persistent in knocking will succeed in

entering." (*Moshe Ibn Ezra*) The Chofetz Chaim offers a novel twist to the question that is asked of every soul that has passed from this world: "Did you fervently await salvation?" Usually this is explained as a reference to the coming of Mashiach. The Chofetz Chaim explained this as a reference to awaiting one's personal salvation. Each and every day, a person must utilize his ability to pray for deliverance from his troubles (*Machane Yisroel II ch. 2*).

Consistency is important. Rabeinu Bachya cites the Gemara, which points out that when a person who regularly attends *shul* fails to arrive one day, Hashem asks for him (*Berachos 6*). Why is his absence significant? It indicates that his faith is incomplete. The prayer he missed could have been at an auspicious moment for the favorable reception of his supplication (*Kad Ha'kemach, The Significance of Prayer*). Each prayer is momentous—none are inconsequential!

Alarm bells began ringing in Mrs. Pollack's head when she received a registered letter from the firm where she had been working for the last twenty years. The letter was brief and to the point: "Due to extensive financial setbacks, the Kolborn Company regrets to inform you that as of today your services will no longer be required. Our lawyer will be available to assist you with all legalities relating to unemployment compensation."

That was it. The letter included no word of thanks for twenty years of devoted service. It was humiliating, to say the least. She felt like a disposable cup being thrown into the garbage.

The truth was, it wasn't totally unexpected. Two months ago Mrs. Pollack had told her husband Reb Nota, a very serious scholar who learned in Kollel full time, that the company was struggling. The office staff had expected that there would be some layoffs. Mrs. Pollack began to suspect that she might be one of those layoffs when she noticed the manager stealing glances at her when she thought she wasn't looking.

Reb Nota and his wife didn't know where to turn. The unemployment allowance would not last for long—and how would they manage after that? Mrs. Pollack was the sole breadwinner for her family of eight children, who were now in danger of losing their parnassa.

Reb Nota slumped down on the couch—which had seen better days—and tried to come up with a plan, but it was impossible for him to think clearly. He got up and headed to the door.

"Where are you going?" his wife asked.

"I can't think straight," he replied. "I'm going to take a walk. Perhaps the fresh air will clear my mind."

A refreshing breeze soothed his flushed cheeks, and Reb

Nota calmed down somewhat. He found himself heading to the house of his elderly uncle Rav Isser Pollack, the patriarch of the family and his closest relative.

Rav Isser was a staunch servant of Hashem, praying and studying with great intensity. He would say Tehillim from beginning to end at the Kosel and other holy places on behalf of the many unfortunates who turned to him for help. On the verse, "Mi yemalel gevuros Hashem yashmia kol tehilaso," he would comment: "Who can destroy the 'gevuros,' the negative decrees of Hashem? Only one who completes all His praise—by saying all of Tehillim at one sitting."

Reb Isser's welcoming smile eased Reb Nota's troubled soul. Over a cup of tea Reb Nota unburdened himself to his uncle. Reb Isser listened attentively, his face reflecting the pain of his nephew.

"What do you plan to do?" he asked when Reb Nota had finished.

Reb Nota sighed. "I have no plans."

Reb Isser could not find the words to comfort Reb Nota. He knew that for every available job, there were at least ten applicants.

"Daven for me," Reb Nota pleaded with his uncle. Reb Isser readily agreed.

Reb Nota and his wife began studying the help wanted ads. As they had suspected, the few good possibilities had many candidates lined up for the position ahead of them. In the meantime, their funds were running out. The children avoided asking for money. All shadchanim were held at bay, for there was not enough money to pay a shadchan—let alone a wedding.

Still, Reb Nota was hopeful. He increased the time he set aside for davening and squeezed in additional Torah study. Each evening he traveled to the Kosel and poured out his heart to his Creator.

Reb Isser would strengthen his nephew's resolve. He told him, "One cannot compare a person who has reviewed his Gemara one hundred and one times to one who has reviewed it only a hundred times. The same is true with tefillah. A person who prays one hundred times cannot be compared to someone who davens one hundred and one, one hundred and two, or one hundred three times.

"Moshe Rabbeinu davened five hundred and fifteen prayers to enter Eretz Yisroel. If he had prayed once more, Hashem would have listened. A person has no way of knowing which prayer is the most significant."

R' Isser would then smile and ask, "Have you davened five hundred sixteen times?" When Reb Nota shook his head, Reb Isser would give him a pat on the back. "What are you waiting for? Go daven."

Occasionally Reb Isser saw his nephew's faith falter. At those times he would tell him, "Look at my Yerucham. He is also suffering a great deal, but he does not despair." Reb Nota knew of his cousin's grief—Reb Isser's son Yerucham had two unmarried sons; the oldest was thirty-three, and the other not far behind. Both good boys, they had still not succeeded in setting up their own homes. Yet Yerucham still retained a joyous optimism. Reb Nota found that he was almost jealous of his cousin's buoyancy.

Inspired by his uncle, Reb Nota returned to the Kosel night after night, beseeching Hashem not to leave him without food for his family. He also included his cousin Yerucham in his tefilos, hoping that Hashem would help them both.

Two months passed this way. Reb Nota was feeling the strain. They were buying the minimum at the grocery store on credit, there was not the slightest indication of a job coming his way any time soon, and he and his wife were growing terribly disheartened.

That night Reb Nota went to the Kosel, as usual. But he found that he could not daven. The words stuck in his throat. "Hashem is not interested in my prayers!" Reb Nota tried davening for his cousin, but again he could not say the words. For four hours he tried to rouse himself to prayer—but he failed every time. Finally, at two o'clock he gave up.

In the throes of despair he headed for home. With his head in a bewildered fog, Reb Nota somehow ended up taking a route that even in better times would have been considered dangerous. He was roused from his depression by a voice with a distinct American accident calling out to him in Yiddish: "Reb Yid! Not an Arab. Reb Yid!"

Startled, Reb Nota suddenly realized where he was—right near Shaar Shechem, by a large Arab neighborhood. He peered at the figure who had called to him, who was clearly not an Arab. As they hurried toward each other, the other man began speaking in a mixture of Yiddish heavily interspersed with English.

The man was an affluent American tourist. He had arrived at Lod Airport a short while before and had taken the first available taxi to Yerushalayim, oblivious to the driver's Arab identity. He had asked to be taken to a good hotel near the old city. The driver, who apparently had no love for the Jewish people, had dropped him off at Shaar Shechem and told him that the hotel was five feet ahead. It didn't take long for the tourist to realize that he was in dangerous territory, and his relief at seeing a fellow Jew was profound.

"I'm grateful that you're here," the tourist concluded. "But tell me. What are you doing in such a dangerous neighborhood in the middle of the night?"

"We'd better get out of the area first," Reb Nota said

hurriedly. "We'll talk more once we're in a safer location."

They quickly walked toward a Jewish neighborhood and flagged down a Jewish taxi. The tourist intended to go to a hotel, but Reb Nota insisted that he come to his house. It was late, and they decided to leave further conversation for the morning.

The next day at Shacharis they both thanked Hashem for guarding their lives. After breakfast, the tourist told Reb Nota a little more about himself.

"I own a company in Florida, and I'm planning on opening a branch in Eretz Yisroel. I need to fill several positions—a manager, assistant manager, clerks and experienced accountants."

Without hesitation, Reb Nota recommended his wife as an accountant with twenty years of experience. His new friend was thrilled with the suggestion, pleased that he had found a suitable employee so quickly. Reb Nota, of course, was equally delighted that his family's financial crisis had been solved.

As the two continued to speak, the visitor disclosed that he had been entrusted with checking out a shidduch for a friend with an older daughter. The prospect was none other than Reb Nota's nephew, his cousin Yerucham's son.

A few weeks later, Mrs. Pollack had begun her new job and Yerucham's two sons were both engaged. With his son and nephew at his side, Reb Isser noted, "One must never tire of praying—for salvation will ultimately appear" (Sheifos pp. 256-265).

Pray At Any Time

We should always be conscious of Hashem's presence hovering over us. Many people have difficulty with this concept—because they misapprehend how closely we depend upon Hashem at every moment of our lives.

One morning the car doesn't start. What happened? The headlights were left on, and the battery ran down. The solution is relatively simple: get a boost from a friend or a mechanic. It doesn't take long for the battery to charge, and then you're free to be on your way. Thank your benefactor, say goodbye, and leave.

Many people transfer this approach to their spiritual devotions. "Help me," this type of person calls to Hashem, "I can't get started." Hashem gives him a nudge, and he starts moving. He's ready to say goodbye, secure in the belief that he can now manage on his own.

This is a mistake. It's not that our batteries are deficient: we don't even have a motor! We are dependent on Hashem to constantly give us "boosts", from birth to the grave. If He were to stand back even a moment we would cease to function. It is therefore vital to constantly turn to Hashem throughout our lives for direction and help.

When Avimelech comments that Hashem is with Avraham in everything he does, it suggests that Avraham called out to Hashem constantly (*Peh Kadosh*).

This was the source of Yosef's success in Egypt. The Midrash informs us that even Potiphar saw that Hashem was with him, for the name of Hashem was always on Yosef's lips (*Midrash Tanchumah Vayeishev 8*. Yosef was always whispering under his breath. This is the meaning of the verse, "And His master saw that Hashem was with him." Rashi explains that the name of Heaven came readily to Yosef's lips. Potiphar saw that Hashem was with him, for Yosef was constantly murmuring requests to Hashem that he find favor in the eyes of Potiphar. When he entered his master's palace he would pray to find favor in his eyes. Potiphar would ask him, "What are you mumbling about?"—fearful that Yosef was uttering magical incantations against him. Yosef explained that he was praying to Hashem to help him fulfill the command (*Be'er Moshe, Ekev*).

As a result, Hashem saw to it that he was showered with success. When Yosef's master would ask for one type of drink and then change his mind and request another beverage, the contents of the cup would change instantly. From juice to wine to water, from hot to cold, his every request was fulfilled. In the end, Potiphar entrusted Yosef with all his keys. This is the meaning of, "And everything he did Hashem insured his success." (*Bereishis 39:4*). With the help of Hashem, miracles became commonplace.

It is possible to reach Hashem at any time. Simply open your heart and speak about anything. No request is too insignificant. Hashem wants us to speak to Him, for He loves us. We are Hashem's beloved; He tells us, "My dove, in the clefts of the rock, in the covert of the cliff, let Me hear your voice" (*Shir HaShirim*).

The Chofetz Chaim did not spend a great deal of time saying Tehillim. He said Tikkun Chatzos only from the seventh of Tammuz until the ninth of Av. What he did do on a regular basis was speak to Hashem in Yiddish.

One of the Chofetz Chaim's friends had a daughter who was suffering from a protracted illness. The Chofetz Chaim went to the place where he usually conversed with Hashem and was overheard saying, "You have accepted my prayers so many times in the past. Please do so again now!" (Dugmah Me'darkei Avi)

The daughter of Rabbi Meir of Constantine and granddaughter of Rav Yaakov Emden spared no expense when it came to her Shabbos preparations. Her husband, a noted scholar, was also quite wealthy, enabling her to purchase the most delectable provisions for Shabbos.

One week she acquired a magnificent fish, and she thanked Hashem for such a royal gift. "Master of the Universe!" she prayed as she made her way home from the marketplace. " You granted me this extraordinary fish in honor of Your holy Shabbos. Please also send me a pious and learned guest to enjoy the fish tonight."

That afternoon a carriage pulled up in front of their door. To the rebbetzin's delight, a distinguished looking man alighted. The guest was invited to stay for Shabbos.

The guest, who was actually Rabbi Yitzchak of Drohobitch, spoke in learning with his scholarly host all Shabbos long. As the day passed, he wondered what he had been sent to rectify in this luxurious setting.

A "query by dream" supplied him with the answer. There was no great task for him to accomplish. He had simply been summoned by Heaven to grant the rebbetzin's prayer to have guests, which she had uttered on her way home from the marketplace on Erev Shabbos.

When Rabbi Yitzchak bid farewell to his hosts, he said to the rebbetzin, "Please, rebbetzin, be careful with your prayers. I was far away, but because of your prayer I was compelled to travel a long distance to spend Shabbos with your family. Please don't do that again!"

Pray for Every Need

The Gemara (*Berachos 8*) cites the verse in *Tehillim* (32:6): "For this all pious ones should pray at every given time." According to Rav Chaninah, we are being advised to pray for a spouse. Rav Nosson says it is a reference to Torah, and Rav Pinchas son of Yair marks it as a reference to death. Rav Yochanan sees the request as a reference to burial and Mar Zutra as a reference to a privy. No request is viewed as insignificant!

A person who lacks wisdom should take advantage of the blessing "*chonen daas*" and earnestly request knowledge, understanding, and intelligence (*See Rashi on Avoda Zara 8, 1*).

A person who feels he has bad *mazel* should beseech Hashem for compassion; as with Osniel son of Kenaz, his poor *mazel* will be transformed to good. The *shofet* Osniel son of Kenaz was born with a poor *mazel*. He prayed for help with his service of Hashem, Torah wisdom, and the opportunity to share his wisdom with disciples. A double blessing was needed: the first to counteract the negative configuration of constellations which caused the poor *mazel*, and the second to grant him his desire (*Malbim, Divrei Hayamim I, 4:10*).

Someone asked R' Chaim Volozhiner for a remedy for anger, irrelevant speech and lashon hara. He replied, "Pray, before these stumbling blocks trip you up. Early in the morning, start your day with a prayer. Beseech Hashem as follows: 'I am about to enter the valley of death, a very dangerous place. Please protect me from all types of sins, specifically the sin of …"

"This prayer should be repeated with great emotion at the end of Shemoneh Esrei" (Hanhagos Ha'Gaon Rebbe Chaim of Volozhin).

The Vilna Gaon would daven for everything, amassing prayers to forestall suffering. He viewed prayers after midnight as most beneficial, and would also repeat his prayers prior to sunrise (Toldos Rav Yosef Zundel of Salant).

The Chofetz Chaim advises that a father and mother should continuously pray that their sons succeed in their learning and become righteous men of good character (Mishnah Berurah 7,110).

A person must pray for every need. If someone's garment is torn and he has no money to replace it, he should pray for a new one. One should pray for all his requirements, large and small. It is true that "Hashem gives food to every living creature,"

(*Psalms 147:9*) but—unlike animals, which are simply given their needs—a human being must receive all of life's necessities through prayer.

The Rebbe Reb Mendel would visit his rebbe Reb Elimelech for months at a time. He would eat at his rebbe's table, and all his needs were cared for.

At one point he decided that it was no longer necessary for him to pray for food, since he was getting everything he needed from his Rebbe. That night, when the shamash gave everyone a bowl and spoon, he somehow overlooked Reb Mendel and neglected to give him a spoon.

Evryone began eating—except for Reb Mendel. The Rebbe Reb Elimelech asked him why he was not eating. "I don't have a spoon," he replied. The Rebbe Reb Elimelech responded, "Now you see how one must ask Hashem even for a spoon!" (Zeved Tov)

Reb Nachman Chazan was once hammering a nail, when the hammer slipped and he hurt his hand. Reb Noson asked him, "Why didn't you meditate before swinging the hammer? You should have prayed to hit the nail and not your hand" (Siach Sarfei Kodesh I 168).

Rav Yecheskel Avramsky was overheard making the following request during Shemoneh Esrei: "Hashem, it is my desire to teach Torah in Eretz Yisroel. But I am incapable of opening a yeshiva on my own. Please plant the idea in the head of a Rosh Yeshiva to offer me a job."

His prayer was accepted soon after his arrival in Eretz Yisroel from England. Rav Isaac Sher of Slobodka offered him a position and he was able to fulfill his dream (Peninei Rabeinu Yechezkel).

Perseverence

There are times when a person feels that he cannot pray. But one should never give up trying. This is the time to reinforce our faith and awe of Hashem. If we continue to pray when our prayers seem lifeless, our prayers will eventually be infused with a Divine life of their own.

Rav Avraham the first rebbe of Slonim derived this concept from a Mishnah: "Whoever upholds the Torah in poverty will eventually uphold it in wealth." Poverty is used to describe someone who lacks understanding. It can therefore readily refer to a person who maintains his commitment to praying, even when he feels a paucity of spiritual enlightenment and no satisfaction in his service. When he persists despite this seeming lack of fulfillment, simply because he is a loyal servant of Hashem, he will ultimately benefit from an illuminating great light (*Ha'osher Sheb'tefillah*).

"If a person were to concentrate on his prayers, the words themselves would give him the energy to pray with all his might" (*Rebbe Nachman's Wisdom 66*).

A man came to the Chofetz Chaim for advice. Earning a living made it difficult for him to set aside time for davening. From morning to evening he was forced to run around, working for the pennies that would put bread on his table. Even while praying he was plotting the next move in his various dealings.

The Chofetz Chaim replied with a parable. When storeowners buy wheat from wheat merchants, they examine the goods by filling a hollow receptacle with wheat and pouring it out on the table. They can then examine the wheat to see if it is free of debris. The quality of the wheat determines its price.

This is the procedure in times of plenty. When there is a drought, however, the wheat is not as carefully examined—for any type of wheat commands a high price.

The Chofetz Chaim noted that in previous generations, when people were more spiritually inclined, each prayer was carefully scrutinized, and only the best were acceptable. But in times of terror and war—in a generation when spirituality is on the wane, and earning a living is so difficult—all prayers are accepted. Even those that would have been rejected in previous generations are welcome. What is most important is that we daven for the sake of heaven (Meir Enei Yisrael I, p. 172).

A person who was not able to pray as he should, once asked the Steipler for advice. He felt very demoralized, experiencing a great deal of anguish and bitterness at his inability to *daven* properly. His prayers lacked enthusiasm and devoutness, and nothing he tried improved matters. And at those times when he *was* able to pray with great feeling and heartfelt devotion—he could not perceive any results. These issues made it difficult for him to continue *davening*.

The Steipler explained that proficiency in *tefillah* is assessed in a far different manner than other types of spirituality. In Torah study, the more a person knows, the greater his accomplishment. With prayer, when someone assesses his *tefillos* as "certain to accomplish a great deal," they may actually be less worthy!

Various types of prayer are characterized as "Prayer of Moshe", "Prayer of Dovid", and "Prayer of the Poor". The *Zohar* notes that the latter prayer is most effective and more elevated than any other, for one who considers himself more needy and humble can pray with additional effectiveness.

When a person is overwhelmed with bitterness and feeling terribly hopeless, he should remember what King Chizkiyahu told the prophet Yeshaya: a person should never give up, even under the most extreme circumstances. He learned this concept from Dovid, who struggled mightily to elevate himself spiritually—but did not despair when confronted with his harsh judgment of his own behavior. King Dovid called out from the depths of his heart, though he knew that he was unworthy of Hashem's compassion. He begged Hashem to recreate a pure heart for him and help him revitalize his spirituality. Hashem responded favorably, and Dovid passed on his experiences with the efficacy of prayer to his descendants (*Pri Tzaddik as cited in Eitzos Ve'Hadrachos*).

In *Tannah Debei Eliyahu* it states that four million, nine hundred thousand angels stand from sunrise to sunset and declare, "Holy, holy, holy is Hashem Master of Legions; the whole world is filled with His glory." An additional four million, nine hundred thousand angels stand in place from sunset to sunrise and declare, "Blessed is the glory of Hashem from His place" (*Tanna Debei Eliyahu Rabbah, 17*).

Why are the praises linked to the movement of the sun, a fixture present only in our solar system? Why do the praises change at different times of the day?

The Slonimer Rebbe offers a beautiful explanation. The service of the first group of angels is in an environment of clear revelation—the equivalent of daylight. They see the presence of Hashem filling the world. The other angels' view of Hashem is obscured by the equivalent of darkness. They therefore call out, "Blessed is Hashem from His place." Though they do not see that He is there, their declaration is no less enthusiastic.

Sometimes the sun appears to illuminate our prayers. At other times, our prayers seem to be said in darkness. Yet as long as we maintain our awareness that the entire world is full of His honor, our service will be linked to the praises of the angels—and then we, too, will sanctify Hashem's name (*Nesivos Shalom*).

Negotiation

The Berditchever Rebbe is remembered for his parleys with the Creator of the World. He would attempt to swap sins for forgiveness, and for a broker's fee he would demand *parnassa* for the Jewish people. When we pray we should similarly employ any negotiating tools at our disposal.

> *During the war years, the yeshiva boys exiled to Shanghai did not catch the virulent strains of the many diseases that were prevalent in that city. There was one exception. One student came down with a bad case of typhus and was close to death. When the mashgiach, R' Yechezkel Levenstein, heard the news, he took a Gemara Shabbos and walked to the aron kodesh. He read aloud, "'If a person is ill and close to death ... even if there are 999 who testify against him and only one testifying on his behalf, he is saved. R' Yossi Haglili says that even if 999 parts of that angel of defense is negative, with only one part positive, he is saved.' Doesn't*

this young man have some heavenly advocates who could rescue him?"

At that moment the boy took a dramatic turn for the better. He eventually completely recovered and became a well-known disseminator of Torah in the United States (Nes He'Hatzalah).

A woman living in the Bais Yisroel section of Yerushlayim has become synonymous with acts of compassion. Many Bais Yaakov schools bring their students to meet this paragon of chesed, so they may observe firsthand how one woman can achieve so much.

According to Rav Chizkiyahu Mishkovsky, this woman was once stricken with a grave disease. The doctors gave her only a short time to live. She began to cry. Turning to Hashem, she said, "Master of the Universe, if I lie in a grave, no one will benefit. I promise that if I walk out of here healthy, I will dedicate myself to sanctifying G-d's name with numerous acts of compassion."

She cried without stop. To the astonishment of her doctors, a short time later she was discharged with a clean bill of health. She began fulfilling her promise and initiated chessed endeavors, which now span the world (Tuvcha Yabiu II, p. 195).

Praying for Others

Rav Zeev Wolf of Strikov clarifies why our prayers are answered first when we pray for others. When a person feels the pain of his fellow Jew he is emulating the characteristics of our Creator, Who feels the pain of all Jews. Someone who puts great effort into following the ways of Hashem is certain to have his prayers answered (*Ha'osher Sheb'tefillah*).

After the funeral of the Sefas Emes, the Avnei Nezer is reported to have said, "It is clear to me why the Sefas Emes passed away from such a rare disease which even the specialists could not diagnose. The Sefas Emes davened for many Jews who had every conceivable illness. Had he been stricken with one of the illnesses for which he had prayed on behalf of others, his prayer would also have been answered for himself. It was therefore necessary for Heaven to create a new illness just for him" (Ha'Modia).

Before Pesach, two chassidim, Michael Aharon Pisravsky and Reb Leib Posen, arrived in Lubavitch at the court of the Rebbe, the Maharash. When Reb Mordechai Aharon went in to speak to the Rebbe, he mentioned his friend Nachman Lipa Seltzer first. He described his poverty, and mentioned that he had sons and daughters who were of eligible age for marriage. He did not leave out a single detail in an attempt to arouse the compassion of the Rebbe for his suffering friend. When the Rebbe gave him a blessing that his friend's distress be diminished, Reb Michael Aharon asked if the Rebbe could give his blessing the assurance of a promise.

He then described his own woeful situation, for he was destitute and in debt. The Rebbe pointed out that despite the gravity of his situation, he was in better shape than his friend Nachman Lipa. "A person knows his own unworthiness," Rav Michal Aharon replied. "He must be happy and not complain."

The Rebbe put his hand over his eyes and meditated briefly. He then said, "Whoever prays for his friend is answered first. May Hashem grant you success."

Within a half a year Nachman Lipa had amassed a fortune. Reb Michael Aharon also achieved unimaginable success.

When R' Leib Posen entered the Rebbe's study, he began with a rundown of his own problems. He then went on to describe the suffering of Reb Shmuel Brin, a friend of his who had lost most of his fortune. "Surely Hashem knows what He is doing," R' Leib Posen concluded, "and the situation can be no other way. Still, we must commiserate with his suffering."

The Rebbe covered his eyes with his hand and said nothing.

After Pesach a fire broke out in Reb Leib Posen's storehouse, and he lost tens of thousands of rubles worth of flax. A fire also broke out in his store, consuming everything. He lost twenty thousand ruble's worth of merchandise—none of which was insured.

A few days later he was back at the Rebbe, pouring his heart out. The Rebbe looked at him with a sorrowful mien. "When Reb Shmuel Brin lost his fortune, you were able to find comfort for his loss and accept the will of Heaven. But when it is your flax and your store, you refuse to accept Hashem's will and can find no comfort."

Reb Leib immediately realized that he had been punished for his callousness toward his friend Reb Shmuel. For two days he wandered about aimlessly, not knowing what to do. Finally he decided to return to the Rebbe and ask for help.

When he first entered the Rebbe's study, he was so overcome that he could not utter a sound. He managed to calm down and asked the Rebbe to help him repent. "I will be more sensitive to the needs of others," he pledged.

"There is a tradition handed down from the Baal Shem Tov," the Rebbe related, "that whoever pronounces something about his friend, either for good or evil, is actually making this pronouncement about himself. If he exclaims that his friend deserves a reward for his good deed, or that he ought to be punished for something terrible that he did, this

verdict is applied to the person himself. One who sits back placidly while another suffers without beseeching compassion for him is his own worst enemy. Hashem will then assess his own shortage of suffering, and may conclude that he ought to have more challenges in his life. But if one prays on behalf of others while suffering his own anguish, Heaven searches for ways to alleviate his suffering. This is the method that enables a person to receive that which he has been praying for others to receive."

Reb Leib listened attentively as the Rebbe continued. "Give three thousand rubles to Reb Shmuel Brin as a loan with no interest so he can buy goods for the Riga fair. Give him the money with a happy heart, buoyed by the knowledge that Hashem has enabled you to do a chessed. Then go to Moscow to purchase supplies for your store. Hashem will replace the damages twofold" (Ha'Tamim Book 7, pp 370 - 371).

In the preface to his sefer on bris mila, Rabbi Krohn tells of a woman he discovered crying at a bris. For this childless woman, attending the various brissim of her friends' babies intensified her pain. Rabbi Krohn suggested that she try to find someone with the same problem and pray that the other woman should be helped. He took her name and gave it to a local yeshiva, asking that the boys pray on her behalf.

One evening about a year later, the woman called to tell him exciting news. "Since that day a year ago, I have prayed every day for another childless woman. Today I had a boy."

After the passing of Rabbi Bulman, the story was told of how a woman approached him to daven for children on her behalf. Rabbi Bulman advised her to pray for his daughter, who was also childless, and arranged for his daughter to pray for the woman. A year later, both women were blessed with children at the same time.

In 1991 Rabbi Aharon Brostovsky of Lakewood and his family went to Moldovia, where he discovered a thirst for Yiddishkeit among young and old alike. When a yeshiva was established in someone's apartment, parents lined up to register their children.

Aside from being an excellent teacher, Reb Aharon was blessed with a good voice. Some months after he arrived, he taught a group of boys a moving tune to the words, "Our brothers, the entire family of Israel, who are delivered into distress and captivity...may Hashem have mercy on them." As the boys sang the tune, one of the teachers explained the meaning of the song.

Tears streamed from Reb Aharon's eyes. He knew that he would soon be returning to his easy life in America, while these boys would remain in Moldavia with little chance of leaving. Reb Aharon raised his hand for silence. "When we were in America we would sing this song and pray on your behalf that Hashem permit you to go free. What do you think of when you sing this song? Whom do you think about?"

There was silence for a few moments. Then Maxime, age 16, replied, "I have reached an understanding that everyone has to build a relationship with Hashem. Everyone must create his own lines of communication with his Creator. If he succeeds, then he has discovered the light. If he fails, he remains shrouded in darkness. It makes no difference whether he is in America, England or Eretz Yisrael. I sing here and pray that all my brothers who find themselves in darkness, wherever they are, should merit to discover the joy of closeness to Hashem" (Sheifos pp. 224-225).

A young man once approached Rav Siberstein with a dilemma. "Our family is in need of salvation. I know of another family in need of the same salvation. Is it appropriate for me to daven for them so I may be answered first?"

The young man wanted to know if the sages' statement would apply to someone whose sole reason for praying for his friend was so he, too, would be granted salvation.

Rav Silberstein cited the Maharal, who focuses on the word "first" in the Gemara, which states that, "a person who prays on behalf of his friend and requires the same assistance will be granted his request first." The Maharal compares this to a person who seeks to irrigate a field by attaching a pipe to a source of water. The intention is to water the field; it is inevitable, however, that the pipe will get wet.

When a person prays for his friend, he becomes the pipe of prosperity. Inevitably some prosperity will remain with him as well. He will be blessed with success "first", just as the pipe gets wet first.

Rabbi Silberstein saw no reason that the young man should not reap the benefits of becoming a channel to success (Tuvcha Yabiu II p. 280).

There are many opportunities throughout the course of the day to pray for others:

At a wedding, pray that the marriage succeed.

At a funeral, pray that the deceased will arrive at Gan Eden quickly and effortlessly.

For someone who needs a *shidduch*, pray that they will find someone appropriate without delay.

When you hear a Hatzolah ambulance pass, pray for the

speedy recovery of the patient.

When you hear that someone has started a new business, pray for his success.

When you hear that someone is childless, pray that Hashem grant him children.

Prayers of the Righteous

If Hashem decreed that a person will endure suffering, what changes when a righteous individual prays for him? How can we understand the power of a righteous person's prayer?

When a *tzaddik* prays for another person, he invests his entire being in his prayers—all of his 248 limbs and 365 sinews. He thinks only of assisting the person in need. In essence, the *tzaddik* has attached that person to his own limbs, which sanctifies him. As a result, his prayers can now be answered.

Rabbi Elimelech explains: "For why does a person endure suffering? It is because he has done a negative action with a part of his body. When the *tzaddik* envelops him through prayer, the limbs of that person become one with the limbs of the *tzaddik*. He is thereby healed from the negativity that he had brought upon himself. Now that his negative action is corrected, the necessity for cleansing through suffering is eliminated" (*Noam Elimelech*).

A visitor waiting to see Rav Moshe Yechiel Halevi Epstein was shocked to hear a loud groan coming from the Rav's room. He rushed inside to see what had happened. The Rav explained, "Someone who just came to see me is in big trouble, and he asked me to daven for him. Since I am davening in his place, I must place his suffering on my shoulders and actually feel it."

A woman who had several children, but had not given birth for a few years, approached R' Yechezkel Levenstein for a blessing. He responded, "Hashem will help you."

She soon became pregnant—but her pregnancy was in jeopardy from the start. Her brother ran to R' Yechezkel for another blessing. His response was somewhat unsympathetic: "Why have you come if all is lost?"

"Is it certain that all is lost?" the woman's brother countered. "There were many similar situations where Hashem helped and everything turned out well. It would not be a miracle. Certainly there is place for prayer."

The mashgiach thought for a few moments, and responded with a gesture. "You grasp the situation well." He prayed on her behalf, and afterward she gave birth to a healthy child (Sheal Avicha Ve'yagedcha).

When Rabbi Yosef Dayan was approached for help, he would say, "Let us pray and Hashem will certainly help."

One day a poverty stricken man bared his hurting heart to R' Yosef. His children lacked even minimal sustenance. "I can help you," R' Yosef soothed him.

The man understood that this was an opportune time to make a request, and he asked for fabulous wealth. "For fabulous wealth it is necessary to pray forcefully over an extended period," Rabbi Dayan explained. "It may take a while. For the moment, let's put that request aside. I will ensure with Hashem's help that you will merit a comfortable living."

A short time later his promise was fulfilled (Od Yosef Chai p. 63).

Mr. Wolf, a wealthy, respectable Jew from New York, had a child who was born mute. Over the years Mr. and Mrs. Wolf came to terms with their son's handicap. But when he came of age, they could not find a shidduch for him. The only girls being recommended were severely handicapped and much older. And even when the Wolf agreed to the various propositions, the girls all rejected him.

Mr. Wolf finally decided to try their luck in Eretz Yisroel.

He visited a friend there who was knowledgeable in the ancient art of palm reading.

"Your son has the ability to speak," he told the surprised father. "I cannot help you, though, for the task is bigger than me. He is a hard nut to crack. Go to Rav Yosef Dayan for help."

Rav Yosef spent a long time scrutinizing the boy. Finally he declared, "By the time you leave Eretz Yisroel you will be engaged." The delighted father left, looking forward to the fulfillment of R' Yosef's promise. In the meantime, the Rav threw himself into praying for the boy—for a shidduch, and for the ability to talk.

Time passed. Only five days remained before their return flight, and there was still no kallah in sight. Mr. Wolf went back to Rav Yosef. "Chacham Yosef, in five days I will be returning to America. Where is the fulfillment of your promise?"

"Postpone your flight for two days," Rav Yosef replied. "This week your son will become a chassan. I believe his kallah is Sephardi of Syrian extraction. Join me tomorrow at the grave of Shmuel the prophet. We will make a rectification ceremony, and all will be well."

When father and son arrived at the gravesite, Rav Yosef took a stone and broke it into seven pieces. He began circling the tomb while saying special prayers. After each circle, he handed a piece of the rock to the mute young man and instructed him to throw it out of the area. When the pieces were all disposed of, Rav Yosef told them that the engagement would take place the following night.

When the Wolfs returned to their hotel that afternoon, a matchmaker was waiting for them with a shidduch—a fine, upstanding girl of Sephardi background. Mr. Wolf was satisfied with his inquiries and quickly arranged for a meeting. The meeting went well, and the girl agreed to a second meeting.

Mr. Wolf explained that their time was limited, since they were leaving the next day. The young woman thought a bit and agreed to make an immediate commitment. The next evening they got engaged.

The wedding was scheduled in New York a few weeks later. The day of his wedding, the chassan suddenly began to speak! The joy of his parents and kallah was immense. Here was the complete fulfillment of Rav Yosef's promise—and a vivid demonstration of the power of his prayer. That night the young man uttered the kiddushin under the chupah in front of the crowd gathered to celebrate this memorable occasion.

He is now a chazzan in a shul in New York, and the couple is very happy (Od Yosef Chai, p. 218).

Different Approaches to Tefillah

Serving with Song

The angels, heavenly beings, and all creatures of this world serve Hashem with song *(Peleh Yoetz).* Our essence too, was composed in song, and that is why the soul, by its very nature, responds with joyous hymns to Hashem.

"Why do children enjoy hearing music?" asks the author of *Livnas Ha'Sapir.* The child's soul remembers hearing the songs of the angels and other Heavenly beings. The music takes him back to the bliss experienced before birth *(Parshas Noach).*

The *Rambam* regards music as a special language, speaking directly to the heart, touching wellsprings of emotion *(Moreh Nevuchim 3, 45).* Combining melody with *tefillah* can stir the heart, arouse the emotions, and intensify the mood one seeks to attain. It is a source of inspiration, enthusiasm and joy. On the verse, "Where singing is heard, there is also prayer" *(Yeshayahu*

26:2), Rashi says song and praise to Hashem should be offered with pleasant tunes.

> *The Mittler Rebbe writes that when a sad person hears a cheerful melody, he immediately becomes happy, though intellectually he does not understand why. When a happy person hears a sad song, he immediately becomes sad. This demonstrates that music affects the depths of the soul, bypassing the intellect (Sefer Ha'Teshuva).*

Song has always been an important factor in Jewish worship. Song lightened the first steps of the newly freed Jewish nation, watching the destruction of Egyptian army at *Yam Suf (Shemos 15:1-20).* They sang their thanks to Hashem for providing water in the desert. Finally, Moshe gave his last will and testament in verse *(Devarim Haazinu).*

Song accompanied the victorious armies of Yiftach and Kings Saul and David returning from battle *(Shoftim 11:34; Shmuel I 18:6-7).* Music also accompanied the progress of the *Aron (Divrei Hayamim I 13:8; 15:16).*

The Kohanim and Levi'im

In the *Mishkan* and later in the *Bais Hamikdash,* song often accompanied the sacrifices *(Arachin 11).* Song lent splendor and dignity, enhancing the service. The loaves of thanksgiving were always accompanied by song *(Shevuous 16; Nehemiah 12).* The offering of the first fruits *(Bikurim 3, 3-4)* featured the sound of the flute, adding fervor to prayer and purifying thoughts for acts of devotion. According to R' Meir, song was an intrinsic part of the offering *(Arachin 11a; Shavuos 2, 2)*.

Of the twenty-four thousand *Levi'im* serving in the *Bais Hamikdash* in King David's lifetime, four thousand praised Hashem with instruments. Those who sang and prayed were appointed as accompanists *(Divrei Hayamim 25:7)*.

The *Mishna* says the chief musician was Hygros, son of Levi, who selected the daily singers. The *Gemara* says of one: "When he tuned his voice to a trill, he would put his thumb into his mouth and place his finger between the two parts of his moustache, so the *Kohanim* staggered backward with a sudden movement." They were overcome by the beauty of the music *(Shekalim 5, 1; Yoma 38)*.

When the *Kohen* stopped pouring wine on the corner of the altar at the wine offering ceremony, two *Kohanim* to his right and left would sound their horns, and the *Levi'im* would join them in song *(Succah, 5)*.

We know the names of many of the musical instruments used in the *Bais Hamikdash*. However, we do not know the nature of the melodies, although some were sung responsively, as in *Tehillim 136*.

Musical Motivation

The *Gemara* hints at the motivating power of music. Rav Huna mentions music being played on ships to encourage sailors to row more effectively, and in the fields to encourage oxen to plow their furrows more vigorously *(Sotah 48a).*

Music lightens our mood and calms our spirits. King Shaul told David to play his harp when overcome by bitterness *(Shmuel I 16:23).* Elisha called for a musician when his anger at King Yehoram caused a temporary loss of his prophetic power *(Melachim 3:15).*

The prophets used music to attain prophetic heights. The *Rambam* writes, "The prophets didn't receive their prophecies at any moment they wished. They first needed to meditate and enter into a joyous spirit... Therefore the prophets would have musical instruments played before them" *(Yesodei Torah 7, 4).*

Some are able to achieve *kavanah* more readily when singing the words of prayer. Song aids memory, making it easier to learn and remember prayers. The author of *Sefer HaChassidim* suggests singing while *davening*. "Seek after melodies and when you pray, say the words in the melody that is most pleasant and sweet to you, and then your heart will be drawn after what you are saying... When you utter a prayer of supplication, use melodies that stir your heart. When you are uttering praises, use joyous melodies so your heart will be full of joy and love toward the One who knows what is in your heart, and you will praise

Him with great love and ecstasy" (*Sefer HaChassidim* 148).

Chassidim harnessed the power of song to arouse strong feelings. Song intensifies emotion, enabling us to pour out our hearts to Hashem. The great Rabbi Aaron of Karlin explains the verse, "Sing from the heights of Amana" (*Shir Hashirim 4:8)* by translating the word *amana* as faith, rather than the name of a place. He says a Jew expresses his faith most fully and joyfully when he sings out freely (*Bais Aharon*).

> *The importance of song to chassidim is reflected in the plaint of Rabbi Pinchas of Koretz, in conversation with Hashem.*
>
> *"Master of the Universe," said Rav Pinchas, "if I could but sing, I would not permit You to live above in the heavens. I would, with my fervent melodies, coerce You to inhabit the earth together with us, Your faithful."*

The *Alter Rebbe* repeated in the name of the *Baal Shem Tov*, "The word is the heart's pen, but music is the soul's pen." The *Chasam Sofer* says that from the moment we begin the melody associated with a prayer, Hashem begins to listen. Any song sung for Hashem's sake can transform severity to kindness *(Sidduro Shel Shabbos, Shaar Shlishi).* The words enhance the brilliance of our prayers' accompaniments.

Melodic Prayers

Prayer, especially *Pesukei Dezimra,* should not be hurried; it should be said with a strong, pleasant voice. The *Tur* says *Baruch She'amar* requires song and melody, since it is a beautiful song *(Tur, Orach Chaim 51).* The *Shulchan Aruch* says *Mizmor Le'Sodah* should be sung, since it speaks of the Thanksgiving sacrifice—the only sacrifice that will not be nullified in the future. The *Shiras HaYam* is another segment of prayer that should be sung with great joy *(Shulchan Aruch, Orach Chaim 51).*

The *Zohar* comments on the verse in *Az Yashir, "Va'yomru Leimor,"* that this song will not be forgotten for all generations. One who merits singing it in this world will merit it in the next world, and will merit using it to praise Hashem in the time of *Moshiach (Zohar 2,54b).*

> *Reb Yisrael Dov Ber of Beliz told the Tzemach Tzedek that he had toiled mightily to understand a concept, which he had finally grasped. Unfortunately, the intellectual breakthrough brought him no satisfaction.*
>
> *He was told that logic could not fully bridge intellectual barriers. The older, more valid means of achieving true insight was to sing while davening.*
>
> *Later Reb Yisrael Dov Ber said that after each prayer, he would be overcome with a longing to learn; and after*

learning, with an even stronger desire to pray (Likutei Diburim Vol. 3 p. 904).

The emphasis of *chassidus* on song in worship has impacted non-*chassidic* congregations. Song has re-established itself as a vital element in modern worship, particularly on *Shabbos* and *Yom Tov.*

Rav Boruch Ber Levovitz was blessed with a beautiful voice and was a talented composer. His beautiful tunes and inspiring mussar themes were stirring. On Shabbos he would pour his soul's love for his Creator into the zemiros, particularly "Libi u'vesari yeraninu el Kel Chai—Blessed are the eyes that witnessed that great heart melting with love" (Marbitzei Torah U'Mussar).

Although song can be vital in serving Hashem, during prayer we must remember to focus on the words. One must be careful that the melody does not overpower content. In the Medieval era, song became so central to *davening* that Rabbinic authorities as early as the twelfth century condemned those who made the prayers secondary to the music, or who entertained a congregation rather than lead it in prayer *(Orach Chaim 53:11; Sefer Chassidim, 418).*

Rav Eliyahu Lopian davened aloud, often singing each word with its proper grammatical inflection. His listeners felt he had interpreted every word. He infused his words with a passion that inspired all. When he fell silent for Shemoneh

Esrei, they were awestruck by the mighty warrior in a posture of total subjugation to the King of Kings (Introduction to Lev Eliyahu).

A Conversation With Hashem

The *Sh'lah Hakadosh* advises each person to pray spontaneously to Hashem for what he needs. Before every effort he should discuss his plans with Hashem, expressing himself as best as he can; only then should he proceed, trusting that Hashem will help him. The moment a joyous thought rises in a man's heart, or he is swept away with love for Hashem's Torah—that moment is auspicious for prayer *(Kav Ha'Yashar).*

This does not conflict with the *Gemara's* recommendation that prayer should be grounded in solemnity *(Berachos 30, 2).* This grounding is required for the *Amidah* prayer, which requires thoughtful preparation. A spontaneous prayer requires no priming: it emerges from an overflow of emotion, erupting into a grand torrent reaching to the Heavenly throne.

Nechemya's conversation with King Darius asking for permission to rebuild Yerushalayim is an example of a spontaneous prayer. The verse begins by telling us that the king asked Nechemya what he wished. Nechemya replied, "And I prayed to G-d in Heaven, and I said to the king, if it pleases the king, and if his servant finds favor in his eyes, please send me to Yehudah, to the city of my father's graves, and I will rebuild it."

Before formulating his response, Nechemya prayed to Hashem to help him succeed in his mission. This demonstrates that we must always ask Hashem for success before embarking on our efforts. Perhaps this is what Kind David meant when he said, "I am (that is, I personify) prayer": it referred to the way he *davened* constantly *(Be'er Moshe, Ekev).*

For Every Need

Children should be taught to ask Hashem for their needs, whether essential or insignificant *(Kuntres Ha'Tzvaah).* An educator once asked the *Chazon Ish* what he should emphasize in his teaching. The *Chazon Ish* replied, "You should entrench in your students a strong belief in Divine providence. The young child will then always be conscious of how Hashem is attentive to his needs. This is the guaranteed road to success, for it fashions a successful adult capable of following the dictum of '*Bechol derachecha de'eihu*—in all your ways know Him'" *(Mishlei 3, 6; Peer Ha'dor).*

> *A young child received a bicycle as a gift from his parents. The next morning he discovered that his new bike had been stolen. He ran to his father, tears overflowing as he gulped out the devastating news.*
>
> *The father gathered the family to pray for the thief to repent and return the bicycle. The children, all very young, had no idea how to compose such a prayer. The father*

supplied the phrasing, and the children repeated after him. Having made their request, they were convinced Hashem would ensure the return of the bike. Even the child whose bike had been stolen went to bed calm and reassured.

Next morning they ran out to look for the bike. They weren't disappointed. On the bike was a note, "Please forgive me. I will never do it again!" It was signed, "The thief."

Their joy was indescribable. Not just for the return of the bike—for the dramatic lesson in the power of prayer. The note is still prominently displayed on the wall to remind the family of this essential lesson (Aleinu Le'Shabeach, Va'yikra p. 110).

The famous blind saint, the Rebbe Reb Shimon of Yaroslav, once visited Belz. Reb Shimon entered the new synagogue and moved along the walls, kissing the stones and bricks. But at one spot he removed his lips from the wall, kissing it again only when he had moved a few steps further.

The Belzer Rebbe was unsurprised by the strange behavior of the visitor. Pointing to the wall where the saint had not kissed, he said, "I wasn't here when this piece of wall was built, and that's why the prayerful touches are missing."

The chassidim who built the shul in Belz had laid stone

upon stone with great devotion. But the bricklayers did not have the ability to breathe their souls into the building or infuse cold stones with spirituality. Only the Belzer Rebbe was capable of this. And the Tzadik Reb Shimon of Yaroslav, was spiritually sensitive enough to notice the omission (Admorei Belz).

Reb Yitzchak of Radzvil composed the following prayer: "We are the children of Avraham who loves You. Therefore, please help me and all of Yisrael by sending us, in his merit, love and faith in Your unity. We are also the descendants of Yitzchak, his only son, who was bound on the altar and who raised himself up for Your sake, resisting the blandishments of the yetzer hara. Therefore, may Your holiness help us prevail over our evil inclinations" (Ohr Yitzchak p. 187).

When Rav Yosef Chaim Sonnenfeld baked matzos he said passages of Tehillim, asking Hashem for the matzos to emerge baked in accordance with halacha.

Meditation

We can meditate at any time: Hashem is always listening. All we have to do is open our hearts and begin.

According to Rabbi Elazar Azkari, one should set aside one day each week to meditate alone with Hashem. "Bind your thoughts to Hashem, as if speaking before Him on the Day of Judgment; speak softly as a slave to his master, or a child to his parent."

Rabbi Nachman of Breslov recommends dedicating quiet moments each day to conversation with Hashem, using our own words in whatever language we know best. Using the language with which we are most comfortable enables us to speak freely.

He views spontaneous personal prayer as the highest and most beneficial level of worship. Prayers should include remorse and repentance, argument and persuasion with words of grace, longing and petition: supplicating Hashem that you become truly worthy of serving Him. Ask that He draw you to serve Him in truth. There is nothing too small or too unimportant for Hashem (*Sichos HaRan 229; Likutei Maharan, Tinuyana, No. 25*).

Elsewhere he writes, "If you set aside a time each day to converse with Hashem you will surely be worthy of finding Him. You may do this for days and years without any apparent effect, but in the end you will reach your goal" (*Sichos HaRan 68*).

Rebbe Nachman himself would start each day by placing the day's activities in Hashem's hands, asking that he do everything according to His will. "This way I have no worries. I rely on

Hashem to do as He sees fit" (*Rabbi Nachman's Wisdom #2*).

Rabbi Pinchas of Koretz strongly urged his children to constantly pray to Hashem at every moment (*Midrash Pinchas*).

The Rebbe Reb Bunim recommended regular prayers to Hashem, requesting all needs—large or small. At any time and in every appropriate place, one should turn to Hashem (*Bais Yaakov VaYetze; Toras Simcha p. 74*).

Asking for Anything

A person's garment is torn, and he has no money to replace it? Pray for a new one! Hashem gives us food, clothing, and everything we need. "Hashem gives food to every living creature" (*Tehillim 147: 9*)—but we receive these necessities through prayer.

Pray to be saved from sin and illness. Pray to be able to fulfill the commandments, to have good character traits, and to use your abilities to their utmost (*Eved Ha'Melech*). Prior to a wedding in the family, our sages would appeal to Hashem to protect them from an evil eye (*Shevet Mussar*).

Pray for the Jewish people! This was the custom of the Rebbe Reb Zusia: as soon as he arose, he would wish a good morning to all of *Klal Yisroel* and request a day of blessing and success for them (*Meor Ve'Shemesh*).

Rabbi Nosson of Nemirov writes, "I once had a slight need for a small, insignificant thing. When I mentioned this to Rabbi Nachman he said, 'Pray to Hashem for it.'

"I was rather astonished to learn that one must pray to Hashem for even such trivial things, especially in a case like this, where it was not even a necessity. Seeing my surprise, Rabbi Nachman asked, 'Is it beneath your dignity to pray to Hashem for a minor thing like this?'" (Sichos Ha'Ran 233)

One Succos Reb Meir Simcha of Dvinsk and his chavrusa encountered a very difficult passage in Tosfos. They could not understand it despite hours of strenuous effort.

Reb Meir Simcha said, "Let's pause for a moment and pray that we merit love of Torah."

"Why pray for love of Torah?" his chavrusa asked in surprise. "Shouldn't we pray to understand Torah?"

Reb Meir Simcha replied with a parable. "A mother leaves her child with a babysitter. The child cries and cries, refusing to be comforted with toys or drinks. When the mother returns, she picks him up—and within moments, the baby is quiet.

"Why does the mother succeed in soothing the child, while the babysitter fails? The answer is simple. Her love for

the baby is so deep that she intuitively knows what is bothering him. She is able to accurately respond to his cry and attend to his needs.

"If we truly love the Torah, it will become an integral part of us, and we will be able to decipher its innermost meanings and understand its intentions. This is why we must pray for love of Torah."

While speaking with others, the Brisker Rav, Reb Velvel, would utter a heartfelt prayer. When a visitor poured out his heart and the Rav needed to find the right words of counsel and comfort, he could be heard repeating verses requesting Hashem's aid (Shearim Be'Tefila, Bitzur).

The daughters-in-law of Simcha Tzadka, who was the mother of Rav Yehudah Tzadkah, asked for the secret of their mother-in-law's culinary success. She explained that when she began cooking she would pray for her dishes to come out tasty, to please her husband. Before Shabbat she would add an additional prayer—that her dishes should be especially delicious in honor of the Shabbat (Ve'zos Le'Yehudah).

Rav Yosef Dayan was recovering from a heart attack at the

home of a disciple. His host ordered a telephone—still an uncommon household item at that time, when telephone service was still in its infancy. It could take years to receive a telephone; to speed up the process, the host considered mentioning that his houseguest was in desperate need of a phone because of his heart condition.

When Rav Yosef was consulted, he said that there was no need to ask for special consideration: "I will get the telephone with my prayers."

Out of gratitude to his host, Rav Yosef prayed at the grave of the Chida daily, saying fifty chapters of Tehillim for two months. Two months later the telephone was installed (Od Yosef Chai p. 146).

It is best to set aside a specific time each day for communicating with Hashem. Otherwise the days pass and are gone, with no time to really sit and think—to consider what we are doing, and whether it is worthwhile to devote our lives to it.

Reb Nachman suggests meditating alone in a room specifically reserved for Torah study, prayer and meditation with Hashem. The best time for this is at night, when the world is free of the daily occupation that distracts and confuses us. It is difficult to achieve self-nullification in conversation with Hashem when the rest of the world is busy pursuing personal vanities (*Likutei Maharan 1, 52*).

Some prefer to meditate in a quiet field, alone with nature. The *Baal Shem Tov* used to practice private prayer and meditation in the forest, where it was quiet and secluded. The atmosphere itself is beneficial to this process.

Rebbe Nachman said, "One who does not meditate cannot have wisdom. He may occasionally be able to concentrate, but not for any significant length of time. His power of concentration will remain weak and cannot be maintained. A person who does not meditate will not realize the foolishness of this world. But one who has a relaxed and penetrating mind will see that all around him is vanity."

For some, talking to Hashem in their own words comes naturally. For others it can be a struggle. The ease of this type of communication varies from time to time, person to person. Yet even our jumble of thoughts and half-formed ideas are important to Hashem. Hashem loves to hear us speak to Him.

Many *tzaddikim* would address Hashem numerous times throughout the day, in grateful recognition of His generosity.

R' Yonasan Shteiff paused briefly during his studies to thank Hashem for the breeze that enabled him to learn more comfortably.

Rav Chaim Shmulevitz walked to the window to thank

Hashem for providing the insight he sought.

When Rav Ben Zion Yadler returned to shul for the first time after recovering from a broken leg, people advised him to express his thanks to Hashem for having healed him.

Rav Benzion replied, "Only now must I feel grateful? Did I have nothing to thank Hashem for before I broke my foot? What about the ability to walk unhindered?" (Hischazkus Be'Tefillah Le'Hashem p. 89).

All Day Long

"*Bechal derachecha daehu, ve'hu ye'yasher orchosecha*—In all your ways know Him, and He will straighten your paths." (*Mishlei 3:6*). Ask for Hashem's help with everything you do throughout your day, and He will insure that you achieve your goals.

The *yetzer hara* convinces most people that it is inappropriate to bother Hashem for small things. Rabbeinu Yona teaches otherwise.

He cites the *Gemara*, which speaks of a thief who applies to Hashem for help as he is attempting to break into a home (*Ein Yaakov Berachos 63*). How is this possible? Although the thief has sinned, his connection with Hashem is not broken. And perhaps he will experience a sense of embarrassment at these negative requests—which will lead him to ask for help in achieving the permissible. This route will inevitably lead him back to his Creator.

Rabbeinu Yona applies these lessons to our own everyday existence. When our numerous small requests are answered, our confidence in Hashem is reinforced, building our faith in Him. This dependent relationship becomes a part of who we are—and we will instinctively continue to turn to Hashem for our needs (*Peer He'dor*).

Lost something? Ask Hashem to help. Going on a trip? Ask for Hashem's protection. And thank Hashem—for falling, and getting up unscathed; for earning a profit in business. Make this a regular habit. You will find that it cements a deep connection and love of Hashem (*Taharas Kodesh*).

Rav Elazar taught that one should *always* pray before a crisis (*Sanhedrin 44*)—which suggests at all times, in every free moment (*Hischazkus Be'tefillah Le'Hashem p. 46*).

Praying for Protection

Throughout the day one should turn to Hashem and request, "Show me Your ways, guide me on the truthful path, fire my heart with fear, and purify my thoughts and heart for Your service" (*Chayei Adam 143*).

When washing the face in the morning, one should bless Hashem for rousing him from his sleep. When washing the eyes, he should request that they not view anything forbidden (*Chidushei U'Beurei Ha'Gra, cited in Kedushas Einayim p. 198*).

Pray to avoid anger or other inappropriate actions and behavior. "Master of the Universe, I am going through a valley of death, a dangerous places. Save me from the *yetzer hara* and from various sins: particularly the sin of …"

If his prayer is sincere, Hashem will protect him (*Rav Chaim of Volozin, Keser Rosh, Letter 73*).

Before eating a meal, pray for continued sustenance (*Shulchan Aruch 166 citing the Zohar*). Before entering the marketplace, pray to be spared from incorrect thoughts (*Keser Rosh of Rav Chaim Volozhiner, Letter 135*).

The Chofetz Chaim wrote a beautiful prayer, requesting help in avoiding *lashon hara* and *rechilus*:

"Master of the Universe, may it be Your will, compassionate and gracious G-d, that You grant me the merit today and every day to guard my mouth and tongue from *lashon hara* and *rechilus*. And may I be zealous not to speak ill of an individual, and certainly not of the entire Jewish people or a portion of it; and even more, may I be zealous not to speak words of falsehood, flattery, strife, anger, arrogance, hurt, embarrassment, mockery, and all other forbidden forms of speech. Grant me the merit to speak only that which is necessary for my physical and spiritual wellbeing, and may all my deeds and words be for the sake of heaven" (*Adapted by Rav Yehuda Zev Segal*).

Pray that you should perceive only good in others, and not their weaknesses (*Reb Elimelech of Lizhensk's prayer before davening*).

Rabbi Shmuel Huminer's *tefillah* for positive listening and reading is worth knowing:

> *Compassionate G-d, help me today and every day to protect my ears and eyes from hearing and reading that which is against Your will: words of lashon hara and rechilus, arguments and unnecessary conversation, and forbidden words.*
>
> *If I heard or read anything that is against Your will, help me forget it all.*
>
> *Protect me that I not hear or read anything inappropriate by accident.*
>
> *May my eyes and ears, heart and brain be sanctified to do Your will with a complete heart.*

The *Yesod Ve'Shoresh Ha'Avodah* has many prayers to be said before the performance of various *mitzvos*. It is also appropriate to make requests after the fulfillment of a *mitzvah*, as we do after *bentching* with the *horachamans* (*Chofetz Chaim on Torah Ki Savo*). Ideally the request should correspond to the *mitzvah* being performed.

The *Rabbeinu Bachya* points out that after lighting the Shabbos candles, it is appropriate for a woman to pray for good children who will light up the world with their Torah.

Davening With A Minyan

The feeling of exaltation that one has when praying with a large group makes praying so much more meaningful. The institution of *minyan* has always provided cohesion in the Jewish community. *Davening* with others carves room in the heart for others' welfare. Most prayers are formulated in the plural, for prayer is not only an individual experience. Prayer is a community effort: man for his friend.

G-d completes the purpose of His creation only when His chosen nation prays for the greater good of their brethren. Only when Jews take responsibility for one another - via communal prayer - will Hashem pour His beneficence on the entire world.

The Magic Number

The need for a quorum of ten is derived from a verse in *Tehillim (68:27)*: "Bless you G-d *bemikhalos*—in full assemblies." The numerical value of the letters "*bemikhalos*," assemblies, is equal to *b'asoroh*, with ten (*Lishmor VeLaasos, p. 36*). The Divine Presence comprises the totality of Ten Emanations (*sefiros*), making sanctification of Hashem impossible with less than ten (*Tikkunei Zohar 18, 35b*).

The verse in *Yechezkel (20:24)* says, "In every place that Hashem's name is mentioned Hashem will come and bless." The Hebrew word for "will come" has a numerical value of ten. Rabbi Yitzchak Luria explains the verse: if you *daven* in an established holy place with a *minyan* of ten people, Hashem will bless you. All the promises Hashem made to the Jewish people apply to them as a whole, not as individuals (*Introduction to Tefillas Chana p. 39).*

The Sages specifically teach that when ten or more pray together, the Divine Presence is with them. For it says in the Psalms, "G-d stands in the congregation of Hashem" (*Tehillim 82:1*; *Berachos 6a*).

The First Ten

A person should always rise early to go to shul, so that he should merit to be counted among the first ten (Berachos 47b). Rabbi Yosef Chaim of Baghdad highlights the significance of being among the first ten to make up the *minyan*:

Every *mitzvah* performed in this world is made known above

by an angel who declares, "Let us praise him." Then the souls of *tzaddikim* bless the good doer.

As a *minyan* forms, the angels announce the first arrival, and he is blessed. When the second man comes, the angels announce the second and the first. When number three arrives, the angels call out the names of numbers three, two and one. And so the angels continue through all ten men. The angels announce the subsequent participants, followed by the names of the core quorum. The first ten men are blessed repeatedly (*Zohar, Terumah p. 131*).

There was a young man who owned a furniture store in a small community. One morning he noticed smoke rising up between the slats of his parquet floor. He quickly ran to the basement to see what was wrong, and soon had his worst fear realized. A fierce fire was raging in the basement. He was unsuccessful in his attempt to extinguish the fire with a portable extinguisher. By the time he ran upstairs, the fire had already spread to the first floor. The furniture was all aflame. He ran to the phone to call the fire department and then returned to his store, to watch helplessly as it burned to the ground.

The fire department finally arrived, but, alas, all they could do was water down the adjacent store to make sure the fire did not spread. His business was gutted. It would be months before he could even dream of opening up again.

A few days after the fire, this young man came to shul and remarked to a friend, "You know, a few days prior to the fire, a fellow came over to me and commented about my late arrival to Minyan. 'You come to shul everyday,' he said, 'but why do you always come so late? You are never there at the beginning of davening."

I replied to him, "'What difference does it make when I come? The main thing is that in the end I am there!' Now I realize that the fire department also came in the end-when my store had already been turned to rubble. It was too late. Hashem showed me that coming in the end is not good enough. It is no different than the fire department. It was too late" (Told by Rabbi P. Krohn).

The first ten to arrive receive a reward equivalent to all those who came afterwards. The *Shechinah,* graces a place where people pray only after there is a *minyan* in attendance. Therefore, it is only the first ten who receive credit for "bringing" the *Shechinah.* The initial reward for those first ten who get the credit for availing the others of the opportunity to have the Shechinah present, is equal to what everyone else receives for praying in the presence of *Shechinah.*

Merits of Many

"*Va'yakatz Yaakov mishnoso va'yomer*—Yaakov awoke from his sleep and he said ..." (*Bereishis* 28:16). The last letter of these four words spell *tzibur*, community. *Tefillos* are answered when they come from a *tzibur*, a congregation, not alone (*Kuzari 3, 19*).

A righteous person praying alone, no matter how sincere his devotions, cannot compare to the prayers of a group. A person praying alone never knows if Hashem is accessible (*Yesod Ve'shoresh Ha'Avoda 2, 7 based on Zohar Vayishlach 167*). When a person *davens* alone the angels collect his prayer. When he prays with a *minyan*, Hashem assembles his prayer (*Mishnah Berurah 101,15*). The Ramban on Shir Ha'Shirim writes that one who prays with a minyan will have his prayer accepted by Hashem, even if he did not concentrate on every word. So great is the power of the tzibbur.

Praying with a *minyan* ensures that Hashem's wrath is deflected. The verse in *Mishlei* says, "In a multitude of people is a king's majesty" (*Mishlei 14:28*). The word used for majesty, *hadras*, can also mean regret or misgivings, as in "*hadrana bi*," a term cited in numerous place throughout the Gemara.

Substituting this alternate translation, the verse reads, "When there is a large congregation of people His Majesty has misgivings." What type of misgivings? Misgivings regarding evil decrees against His people. When supplicants pray to Hashem en masse, they arouse Heavenly compassion, mitigating the evil decrees (*Meor VeShemesh)*.

Concealing Blemishes

Unlike the *tefillah* of the individual, whose prayers and deeds are scrutinized before being accepted by Hashem, a congregation's prayers are not subject to this process (*Zohar 1:234b*). The combined good deeds of ten people please Hashem, for their *mitzvos* compensate for and complement one another (*Kuzari 3, 19*).

> *Two different towns were eligible for royal privileges, and the king had to choose between them. Both towns sent gifts to the king to win his favor—but each chose vastly different methods.*
>
> *The members of the first town sent gifts individually, at different times. As each gift arrived, the king examined it—and usually managed to find fault with it. The second town sent a single, large shipment with various gifts. When the huge package arrived, the king was impressed by the volume and enormity, and did not examine each gift individually. Ultimately, the second town won his favor.*

A person praying alone is unattached to the Oneness of Hashem. But an individual praying among others joins in their unity and thus becomes unified with Hashem. Even wicked people can count themselves in the congregation, for Hashem does not reject the prayers of a group (*Rambam, Laws of Tefillah, first halacha*). Since the entire *klal* is one unit, to reject the wicked man's prayer is to reject the prayer of the righteous.

In any given moment, even if some individuals are not paying close attention to the words they recite—at least one of the quorum is praying with devotion (*Otzar Nechmad, as cited by Sifsei Renanos, p. 168*). The protective shield of a *minyan* helps safeguard our efforts to pray with the appropriate concentration (*Nidchei Yisrael, ch. 5*). Only select individuals can pray perfectly and with pure intent. The average individual's lack of *kavanah* is made up by his neighbor's zeal; together, their prayers will rise to heaven (*Kuzari 3: 17-19*).

Riding On the Merit of One

A group of loyal admirers prepared a wreath for their king. A poor man came along and wove his contribution into the wreath. The king said, "It is because of this poor man's contribution that I am ready to accept your gift." (Midrash Eicha 3:3). The same applies to minyan: it may be the prayer of a single individual that propels all the tefillos heavenward.

When a person prays for help in an area where he has made no serious effort, his prayer is rejected (*Awake My Glory*). For example, only if one has made a conscious and concerted effort against evil speech can he sincerely beg of Hashem, "*Elokai netzor leshoni me'ra*—Hashem, guard my tongue from evil!" An individual reciting these words cannot be certain that his attempts at guarding his tongue will ensure Heavenly intervention. But members of a group can be confident there are individuals in the *minyan* who are truly working on observing sanctity in speech. Within the *minyan* one can apply for and expect help in avoiding the pitfalls of this terrible sin (*Introduction to Tefillas Channah, p. 38*).

REINFORCING OTHERS

A wealthy merchant must deliver a parcel of valuables to his father, who lives on the other side of the ocean. Does the merchant journey alone? Never! He hires strong and capable guards to travel with him, for he knows robbers lie in wait, ready to ambush him. Accompanied by his guards, the merchant safely delivers the treasure.

Every individual has a treasure: his *tefillos*. He tries to dispatch them to Hashem, but the robbers, destructive angels created by prohibited speech during prayers, keep trying to intercept them. To protect the *tefillos*, one must hire guards: *minyan* and *beis hakenesess*. The quorum and the synagogue act as sentries for *tefillos*.

A splendid bird was spotted in the kingdom. He perched atop the tallest tree in the land, so high none could hope to reach it. When the king was informed of the existence of this marvelous specimen, he ordered that it be brought to him. "Stand on one another's shoulders, until the highest man can reach that bird!" ordered the king.

The king's men assembled, determined to fulfill his majesty's wishes. Each man balanced precariously on the shoulders of the man below. As the tower of men grew, the servants near the bottom were distracted and started to wander off. As soon as they moved, however, the entire column collapsed, injuring several of the men.

The men had doubly failed the king. Even greater than his desire to see the bird was his wish to see his men completely united in the pursuit of a single goal (Ohr HaChochma 4).

The quality of a *mitzvah* performed by a large group far surpasses the quality of the same *mitzvah* performed by a single individual (*Bais Elokim, Shaar Tefillah ch. 11*). The onus is upon every individual to cleave to the larger community to *daven*. If not, he forfeits the majority of his reward (*Zelach, Berachos 26*). Hashem desires the unity of His people in prayer. Each member of the congregation stands on the shoulders of his neighbor. If just one member strays, the entire congregation collapses.

R' Eliyahu Dovid Rabinowitz wrote that *davening* alone is like not *davening* at all (*Nefesh David 13*). When one prays alone one is more likely not to *daven* with *kavanah*. He will complete his prayers hurriedly to get on with his day. Rarely will he feel inspiration. *Kavanah* improves as a member of a *minyan*. The mere presence of others restricts stray thoughts. The *chazzan's* moving melody, the sight of the holy Torah scrolls, and the intense devotion of a fellow worshipper can all inspire more fervent prayer (*Introduction to Tefillas Channah p. 39; Rimazei Shir Hashirim*).

Setting An Example

A wise person arranges his day around the three daily prayers. He will go to sleep on time without whiling away the late hours of the night with meaningless activities, for that will impair the next day's performance (*Kisei David, Derush 18*).

One who never fails to *daven* with a *minyan* demonstrates the importance of *tefillah*. A child who sees his father value his prayers learns to take his own prayers seriously. An adult who scrupulously attends *minyan* is usually the child of a father who was himself meticulous in this *mitzvah*.

Every Jew readily able to visit the House of Hashem must adopt the grateful attitude of King David. King David valued the privilege of prayer. "And I, as a result of Your compassion, come to Your house." In his great compassion, Hashem enabled King David to come. The favor is to the benefit of the worshippers, not to the benefit of Hashem. In the hospitals and old age homes, hundreds of patients are confined to their beds, unable to walk or even move. How much they would pay for the opportunity to *daven* in a real *shul* - even for one prayer!

According to the *Zohar*, *davening* alone is dangerous (*Part I, p. 234*). To mitigate the danger when forced to pray alone, one must pray with a broken and contrite heart, always remembering to first praise Hashem (*Devash Lefi of the Chida, Tefillah*). He must make an effort to pray with intense concentration, laden with awe and self sacrifice, to propel his prayer heavenward with great force. Because *davening* in this manner is difficult, it is worth making the effort to join a *minyan* (*Ruach Chaim* on *Avos* 2, 13; Sulam on *Zohar Vayechi 234*).

"And Yaakov was very fearful" (*Bereishis 32:8*). When our forefather Yaakov was separated from his children, he became terribly afraid. With his children, he had nothing to fear, for their combined prayers formed a multi-strand exaltation of Hashem. But when he prayed alone, his prayers were not as well received.

Yaakov, the most exalted of the patriarchs, was nervous about his solitary prayer being accepted. How should a Jew of our generation feel, *davening* alone while the *shul* lies just around the corner? (*Rosh HaGiva*)

Coinciding With Minyan

Communal worship is so important that if one is unable to attend a communal service, it is best to pray privately at the same time as the congregation is praying. King David pleads in Psalms, "May my prayer to You Hashem be at a favorable time" (*Tehillim 69:14*). When is the most favorable time? Prayer is most welcomed by Hashem when the congregation is also *davening* (*Berachos 8a*).

R' Yitzchak once asked R' Nachman, "Why doesn't the master daven in shul?"

"I cannot come to shul," R' Nachman replied.

"Let the master gather ten people and daven with them in his house," suggested the talmid.

"It is too difficult for me."

"So let the master ask the Reader to inform him of the time when the congregation davens," offered R' Yitzchak (Berachos 7b).

Spare No Effort

Every step taken toward *shul* is rewarded. The more steps, the greater the reward (*Shemiras HaLashon*).

> *A noted rabbi once met R' Yechezkel Sarna leaning heavily on his stick, hobbling slowly toward shul. It seemed unlikely that the elderly Rav would find a minyan for maariv at that late hour. "For the slight chance of finding a minyan, it's still worth the effort," responded Rav Sarna.*
>
> *Years later, whenever it was difficult for the rabbi to find a minyan, he would recall the elderly Rav Sarna dragging himself to shul—and that would inspire him to make the*

additional effort.

As long as the Steipler, Rav Yaakov Yosef Kanievsky, was still able to walk for four amos, he continued to make a great effort to get to shul. Benches were set up along his route so he could rest every few minutes (LeShichno Tidrishu).

On the last Thursday of his life, Rav Shlomo Zalman Auerbach was determined to daven shacharis in shul. He refused to trouble the bochurim to join him at home for a minyan. His attendant tried to prevent him from going. The rosh yeshivah was so weak, he wobbled, but he could not be persuaded to daven at home.

As they walked slowly to shul, Rav Shlomo Zalman commented that he felt a terrible cold penetrating his body; his legs were heavy as stones. The attendant wanted to return but Rav Shlomo Zalman insisted that he must daven with a minyan. After completing his prayers, the rosh yeshivah could barely make it home. It was the last prayer he davened with a minyan, a prayer said with great self sacrifice (HaMaor HaGadol).

Even a raging snowstorm did not prevent the elderly Rav

Yehudah Tzadka from venturing out to daven with a minyan. When he arrived, the others were shocked. How could a man of his age walk in the slippery snow? "I fell only three times," he announced proudly. "I fell, and I got up and moved on. I fell again, but I kept on moving" (Vezos LeYehudah).

While recovering from a severe illness, Harav Shalom Schwadron went to live at his daughter's home. One Shabbos afternoon after the meal, Rav Shalom, suddenly very tired, went to nap. A few minutes later, he leaped out of bed and went to sit at the table.

"Your mother has left the house," Rav Shalom explained to his grandson. "I don't remember if I asked her to wake me for mincha. I'm afraid that if I fall asleep now, I may not wake up in time for mincha."

But Rav Shalom's daughter had returned, and had gone to her room to lie down. By the time Rav Shalom realized she was home, she was asleep, and Rav Shalom would not think of rousing her to ask her to wake him for mincha.

Instead, he waited until his daughter woke from her nap. At that point the elderly Rav Shalom had been battling exhaustion for five hours. He asked her to wake him in a half an hour and lay down to rest, completely spent. Half an hour later, when his daughter woke him, Rav Shalom rose immediately, as if he had enjoyed a long nap.

Throughout R' Chaim Yosef Dovid Azulay's extensive travels on behalf of the Jews of Eretz Yisroel, he made exhaustive efforts to seek a minyan. In his travelogue he writes of his search for shuls and the pains he took to gather a quorum of ten. When he succeeded in joining a minyan which he had struggled to bring together, he was overjoyed (Maagel Tov).

Spare No Expense

All his life, Rav Chaim Volzhiner was vigilant about *davening* with a *minyan* (*Etz HaChaim*). He often declared that one who is careful to always *daven* with a *minyan* will be helped by Heaven to find a *minyan* (*Bechol Hakasuv leChaim, p. 122).*

Once R' Chaim was visiting a remote hotel, where there was no minyan. As the afternoon bore on and mincha time approached, he dispatched three messengers to three nearby communities to collect men for a minyan. They returned unsuccessful. R' Chaim still waited until the last possible moment, in case a wayfarer passed on the scarcely traveled road to complete their quorum.

R' Chaim Palagi would pay people to accompany him on

his travels to villages with a small Jewish population, so he would never have to daven without a minyan (Tzavaas Chaim).

When Jews in Yerushalayim were confined at home by a British imposed curfew, Rabbi Tzedaka Chotzin rented an apartment for a minyan of people to live. He supported them for the duration of the decree just so that he could daven with a minyan.

When the great mekubal R' Mordechai Levaton was too old and weak to go to shul, his congregants organized a minyan in his house. One winter day a huge storm raged, and no one came to daven. Terribly distressed, the tzaddik sent his attendant to seek a minyan. He returned emptyhanded. "No one would venture out in this dreadful weather," the attendant explained.

R' Mordechai Levaton withdrew his meager savings from his hiding place. It was just enough to pay for his shrouds and to give to those who would study Torah in his memory after his death. "This is all I have," he told his attendant. "Offer it to the people who usually come to daven here."

Rabbi Chaim Mordechai Roler, the Gaon from Neimetz, was never seen davening alone even when traveling far from home. During times of persecution, when it was dangerous for a Jew to be seen in public, he continued to seek out a minyan. His publication "Barchi Nafshi" tells of one such outing.

Prior to his departure to Kishinev, R' Chaim Mordechai sent a telegram to his friend, requesting that he gather a minyan for his anticipated arrival late the next evening. When he arrived at the train station, he hired the quickest wagon to take him to the home of his friend. As soon as he walked in, they began the maariv prayers.

"Did the Gaon have yahrtzeit tonight?" the host questioned after davening was over.

"No," replied the Gaon. "I invested the money and effort simply so I could daven with a minyan" (Marbitzei Torah Me'olam HaChassidus).

At great financial expense, R' Moshe Aharon Stern always arranged his flight schedule to maximize his chances of praying with a minyan. On one visit abroad, he learned late at night there would be no minyan the next morning. He ordered a cab to transport him to another city several hours away where he knew he would find a minyan.

The first time he went to Amsterdam, R' Moshe Aharon had no idea where the shul was. Armed with directions from a helpful acquaintance, he embarked on his search for the morning minyan. But with snow falling furiously, R' Moshe Aharon was soon lost. "Hashem, I've worked so hard to find a minyan," he prayed. "Please don't let my efforts come to naught!"

No sooner had he finished his prayer when a car pulled over and a Jew rolled down the window. "What are you doing wandering around at this hour in such miserable weather?" the man asked.

"I'm looking for a minyan," replied Rabbi Stern.

"Get in. I'm headed for Shacharis, too."

Rabbi Stern was the tenth to arrive, completing the minyan (HaMashgiach MeKaminetz).

"One o'clock in the morning? And I didn't daven maariv yet!" the mashgiach of Kaminetz berated himself. During the regular yeshiva maariv, the mashgiach had been attending to an important matter. Now he picked up the phone to summon a taxi. "Well, if I have to pray alone, at least I should pray at the Kosel."

Under the dark carpet of the night sky, the Kosel plaza is usually deserted. But when the taxi dropped the mashgiach off at one-thirty in the morning, a group of French yeshiva boys had gathered before the Kosel's large stones. Their flight had just arrived only a couple of hours earlier. Straight from the airport, they came to the Kosel for maariv. The mashgiach joined the minyan, marveling at the Divine Providence, which had manifested itself so clearly (HaMashgiach MeKaminetz).

Many years ago the community in Hebron dwindled drastically. The residents did not even comprise a full quorum. Only when there were visitors did they have a minyan.

One year, as Yom Kippur approached, they were particularly troubled. "Where are we going to get a minyan?"

On Erev Yom Kippur, they were still one Jew short of the required ten. The small group of Jews scattered toward the main road, hoping against hope that somehow a tenth Jew might miraculously arrive to complete their minyan.

Just as the sun was about to dip down past the horizon, a stranger appeared. Dressed in old, plain clothes, he carried a small sack on his humped back. The tiny assembly joyously ushered him into the sanctuary, and the Yom Kippur service began.

Yom Kippur eve, the guest stayed up all night, deep in

meditation and prayer. Not wishing to disturb, no one attempted to engage him in mundane pleasantries. No one learned the stranger's name or origins on the holy day of Yom Kippur. But after the fast was over, everyone was eager to host the special guest. To avoid quarreling they drew lots to see who would take the guest home to break the fast.

The shamash of the shul was overjoyed to win the honor. He approached the guest and introduced himself. But the guest divulged nothing of his identity aside from his name: Avraham. As they strolled home, the shamash contented himself to carry on a one-sided conversation. He prattled on noisily until an ominous stillness quieted him. The shamash looked around fearfully. He was alone! The guest had disappeared!

The shamash frantically ran this way and that. He retraced his steps and told the others what had happened. The Jews of the settlement searched everywhere but could not find the guest. After hours of searching they all returned home, sad and disappointed.

During the shamash's fitful sleep that night, Avraham appeared in his dreams. His face was radiant and he was beautifully attired. "Do not worry, my friend," he assured the shamash. "As you see, I am perfectly all right. I am your father Avraham, sent to this world to help with your minyan."

A Rewarding Practice

The *shul* is regarded as the House of G-d. Those who attend are Hashem's favored guests; those who do not spurn His favor. Regular attendance at *shul* is accordingly rewarded with long life.

A very old woman said to R' Jose son of Chalafta, "I have grown too old. My life has lost its taste, for I can neither eat nor drink. I would gladly change this troublesome life for immediate death!"

R' Jose asked, "In what merit have you lived so long?"

She replied, "I have always been accustomed to leaving everything, even the most pleasant occupation, and going to shul early each day."

"Do not go to the synagogue three days in succession," he counseled. She obeyed his suggestion. On the third day, she fell ill and died (Yalkut Shimoni 4).

In the times of the Gemara, R' Yochanan wondered why there were so many elderly citizens living in Bavel. Residents of Eretz Yisrael were blessed with longevity, but in what merit did the men of Bavel live such long lives? The seniors of Bavel habitually arrived to *shul* early and earned long life.

R' Elya Lopian attributed his own longevity to always being

among the first ten forming the *minyan* (*Introduction to Lev Eliyahu*).

The *Maor VeShemesh* derives the significance of praying with a minyan from the verse, "You shall worship Hashem your G-d (in the plural) and he shall bless your bread and your water (singular), and I shall remove illness from your midst (Shemos 23, 25).

If one prays communally, the effect will be so powerful that the individual will be blessed with a livelihood that is easy to come by, and good health. Each *minyan* member will also be blessed with spiritual success, for bread and water are both symbols of Torah study (*Mishlei 9:5*).

> *R' Shalom worked as a mashgiach at a resort in Shoresh, high up in the Judean mountains. Since the hotel clientele was not observant, scraping together a minyan for mincha was one of the most difficult challenges of his position. Every afternoon R' Shalom would scavenge the hotel environs for men willing to join a minyan.*
>
> *One afternoon he spotted a farmer delivering produce to the kitchen. It was quite clear from his bare head that he hadn't come to Shoresh looking for a place to daven mincha. Armed with his strong commitment to minyan, R' Shalom was willing to give it a try.*
>
> *"My name is Shalom," he introduced himself to the*

stranger. "I'm the mashgiach here, and we're looking for a tenth man to join our minyan for afternoon prayers."

"I'm Yoram. What did you say you're looking for?"

The puzzled expression on Yoram's face told Shalom that this would require more explanation. R' Shalom started from the beginning. "We need a minimum of ten adult Jewish men in order to pray together," he explained.

Yoram listened patiently. Although pretty much in the dark, the man was still willing to do someone a favor. He obligingly followed Shalom inside the hotel where eight other men waited to start Ashrei. "I've got our tenth man," R' Shalom announced. "Our friend Yoram here is willing to help us out."

"Todah rabbah," they greeted him. Ashrei immediately commenced, and mincha was underway. Before the sparse minyan reached Shemoneh Esrei, an eleventh man appeared, this one wearing a yarmulka. Yoram didn't know much about mincha, but he could count. Since there were now ten men without him, he correctly assumed his presence was no longer required. He slipped out the door and left.

At the time the incident hardly seemed remarkable. In fact, R' Shalom forgot all about it. Most likely so did Yoram.

Ten years passed before R' Shalom recalled that afternoon

in Shoresh. In a vivid dream, R' Shalom saw a vaguely familiar figure whose face glowed with unbounded joy. The man drew nearer and asked, "Do you remember me? I'm Yoram the farmer, who agreed to join your minyan for mincha that day in Shoresh."

The event came back to R' Shalom. "Ah, yes," he said. "Now I remember."

"I can't thank you enough for what you did for me," Yoram said in the dream. "A month ago I passed on to a better world. The reward I was given for agreeing to be the tenth man for mincha is greater than anything I can describe to you. And because I was willing to help you then, I've been allowed to come back and ask you to help me."

R' Shalom listened silently to the smiling Yoram as he elaborated on his request. "I left only one son behind in this world. He knows nothing about tefillah, not even the importance of saying Kaddish for me. He lives in Yerushalayim. I beg you to go and convince him to recite Kaddish in my memory." Yoram gave R' Shalom the exact address of his son, and then he disappeared.

In the morning, R' Shalom recalled the dream and all its details. It had seem so real. Could it possibly be true? It wouldn't be so difficult to determine whether it was just his imagination or not, R' Shalom reasoned. All he had to do was to go to the address Yoram had given him in the dream.

If he found Yoram's son living there, all doubts would be resolved. He would plead with the son to honor his father's last wish and recite Kaddish for him.

R' Shalom made the trip to Yerushalayim. He found the address and knocked on the door. It took only a few words to establish that he had indeed found Yoram's son! The dream was true; both R' Shalom and Yoram's son agreed on that.

Now R' Shalom started to explain the significance of saying Kaddish. When he told of the request in the dream, the son agreed to do this one last chessed for his father. R' Shalom was elated that his mission was a success. And surely Yoram was happiest of all. In the merit of the few minutes he sacrificed to complete a minyan, he gained untold reward in the next world (Yated Ne'eman).

An Evil Neighbor

One who avoids the house of Hashem arouses His anger and brings suffering upon himself. The Gemara says in the name of Rabbi Yochanan, "Whenever Hashem comes to a *shul* and sees that there is no *minyan*, He becomes angry" (*Berachos 6*).

Resh Lakish adds, "Whoever has a synagogue in his town and does not worship there is dubbed an evil neighbor; for it is said, 'Thus says the L-rd, as for all My evil neighbors that touch the inheritance which I have caused My people Israel to inherit, I will pluck them up.' What is more, he brings exile upon himself and his children, for it is said further, 'I will pluck them up from their land and will pluck up the house of Judah from among them'" (*Berachos 8*).

Why is a person dubbed an evil neighbor for not attending his local *shul*? The *shul* is like Hashem's house. Just as a person likes to visit his friend, he should want to visit Hashem in His home as well. When he ignores the opportunity to spend time in Hashem's place, he is called a bad neighbor.

By avoiding *shul*, he indicates that he is uninterested in joining those gathered to pray to Hashem. He is opting for a more distant relationship with his Creator (*Nesiv HaAvodah 4).* As he is uninterested in joining his neighbors in worship, he is befittingly exiled and physically separated from them.

Things are very black for the bad neighbors in the next world, too. The *Zohar* informs us of the second division of *gehinnom*, *Shachas*, where it is pitch-black darkness, with no compassion. The people who have a *shul* in their city but never pray there are condemned to this part of *gehinnom* (*Zohar Chadash, Rus, p. 33*).

Leaving his birthplace behind, an elderly man followed his pioneer children to the land of Israel. To his horror, the man discovered that his children were no longer observant. Nevertheless, the grown children insisted that their elderly father live nearby.

Cholon, he soon learned, was a spiritual wasteland. There was no shul, no mikvah, and certainly no yeshiva. The lack was hollowing a hole in his heart.

The new immigrant paid a visit to the Chazon Ish to pour out his woes. "All my life I was careful to daven with a minyan. Who would ever imagine that when I arrived in our holy land I would end up in a place with no minyan? Should I leave my children and relocate to a more religious community?"

The Chazon Ish questioned his petitioner closely. "Were you truly careful never to daven without a minyan? Is a religious environment vital to you?"

"What is my life worth without these basics?" the man replied fervently.

The Chazon Ish was convinced he was truthful. He advised the man to remain in Cholon. "If your desire for a minyan and other spiritual amenities is truly heartfelt, then they will happen. You will have your shul, even in a spiritual wasteland. It will be a large shul, which will positively influence the entire community."

The man stayed in Cholon, and within a short time, a newly founded shul blossomed. A yeshiva even sprouted in town! "All this is in the merit of the Chazon Ish," the old man would recount with satisfaction (Peer HaDor II, 140).

Seeking a Minyan

A traveler who has arrived at his destination is obligated to travel on for four *milin*, or retrace his steps up to one *mil* to find a *minyan* (*Shulchan Aruch 90, 16*). At home, one must seek a *minyan* within a *mil* radius of his house (*Mishnah Berurah*). Contemporary *poskim* have determined that one should travel 18 minutes by car to find a *minyan.*

R' Shlomo Zhviller was especially careful with the halachic requirements related to tefillah. Since it was unusual for R' Shlomo Zhviller to travel without an entourage, davening with a minyan was never an issue.

On one late night trip home from Meron, R' Shlomo was feeling unwell. He dissuaded his followers from joining him and traveled unaccompanied, save for a single attendant. Thus he arrived in Jerusalem at an advanced hour without a minyan for maariv.

Convinced that a quorum was not to be found, his attendant davened alone. But R' Shlomo would not concede. Ignoring the lateness of the hour and his ill health, he combed the shtieblach of Meah Shearim to gather ten men to pray with him. Much to his delight, a minyan was assembled. R' Shlomo prayed maariv with immense joy that night, his illness completely forgotten (Rabbi Shlomo of Zhwill).

Someone once posed the following question to Rav Moshe

Feinstein: Should a scholar learn Torah at night, at the expense of missing a *minyan* in the morning? In response, the *rav* stressed the importance of *davening* with a *minyan* (*Orach Chaim Part two 27*).

> *Rav Moshe Feinstein himself rejoiced in the privilege of davening with a minyan. He was happy when he moved to a new apartment further from the yeshiva. Now he could earn extra reward for walking to perform a mitzvah!*
>
> *While Rav Moshe vacationed in the Catskills, a driver would pick him up every morning to transport him to davening. One morning Rav Moshe waited and waited, but no driver came. Rav Moshe set out on the three-mile trek to a nearby camp. The journey was primarily uphill, but that did not deter the seventy-four-year-old tzaddik.*
>
> *Just as the minyan was about to read the Torah, Rav Moshe walked in. Someone later asked why he had made the effort to come when he knew that he would miss most of davening. Rav Moshe answered, "Should I miss the reading of the Torah?"*

Conducting business prior to *davening* is forbidden. If a person will definitely lose a lot of money due to his *davening* with a *minyan*, he is permitted *daven* alone. This does not apply to losing the *opportunity* to make a lot of money. In that case, he should forgo the transaction.

Bedecked in his tallis and tefillin en route to shul, Rabbi Zalman Mirles was approached by a jeweler who wanted to sell him a number of exclusive precious stones. "Please, come with me to my house and we can arrange an agreement," the jeweler invited Rabbi Mirles.

But Rabbi Mirles declined. "After davening," he insisted.

Rabbi Mirles could have prayed alone, rushing through his prayers so he could conduct the negotiations immediately after davening (Mishnah Berurah 90, 29). But he prayed slowly and intently, with a minyan.

When Rabbi Mirles returned home, he learned that the stones had been sold to another dealer who made a huge profit on the transaction. Rabbi Mirles was overjoyed. "Look at the sacrifice I made to pray with a minyan!"

Eager to welcome the Chasam Sofer as their new rav, the Mattesdorf community arranged a gala reception in anticipation of his arrival the next day. But the Chasam Sofer unexpectedly changed his travel plans. If he followed his itinerary, calculated the rav, he would arrive in Mattesdorf too late to daven with a minyan.

Instead, the Chasam Sofer traveled through the night, arriving at his new home at sunrise. Despite their disappointment, the Jewish community could only admire the righteousness of their newly appointed leader, who placed the honor of Hashem before anything else (Chut HaMeshulash).

Consideration for Others

A person may enter *shul* and proclaim fervently, "*Le'shem Yichud*—for the sake of Hashem!" before donning his *tallis*. He may recite the blessing with joyous enthusiasm. But then he throws the *tallis* over his shoulders, paying no attention to the innocent people being swatted by his fringes.

He may sing *Pesukei Dezimra* with great gusto, building a climax of emotion as he approaches "*Nishmas kol chai*". But his cries are so loud that the *chazzan* cannot continue. He may stand *Shemoneh Esrei* longer than the *rav*, whispering the blessings with focused *kavanah*. But he stations himself near the door so no one can pass until he is finished.

This lack of consideration is unacceptable behavior. We must emulate the behavior of Hashem. Though Hashem resides in the upper spheres, though He is exalted and holy, He lowers Himself to see what transpires in this world. Even when we mortals are spiritually elevated, we must interact circumspectly with our peers, always showing consideration for others (*Lev Shalom pp. 361-362*).

Chorus of Holiness

We no longer have a *Bais HaMikdash*, the sacrifices, or the *Urim VeTumim*. The only visible remnant of formal worship of Hashem is the *shul*. To prove ourselves worthy, we must put forth our best effort to join this forum, especially to answer to *Kaddish*, *Kedusha*, *Borchu* and a generous number of *Amens* (*Kisei David, Derush 18*).

The benefits of each response to *Kaddish*, *Kedusha* and *Borchu* are breathtaking (*Shemiras Halashon II, 9*). Participating in *Borchu* creates crowns for Hashem. Holiness spills over on those who pronounce the words of *Kedusha* at a *minyan* (*Mishna Berurah 125, 4 based on the Ari HaKadosh*). It creates a sanctification of Hashem among the Jewish people, enabling the fulfillment of a Biblical obligation (*Vayikra 22:32*).

R' Chaim Vital suddenly developed severe pains in his eyes. "Perhaps my teacher can explain why I suffer so," he entreated his Rebbe, the great Arizal.

"It results from observing me while I recite Shema, Modim, Kedusha," the Ari explained. The dazzling lights emanating from the Ari's devotions had injured R' Chaim's eyes. He began to avert his eyes at those times and was immediately cured (Shaar Mitzvos, beginning of Parshas Eikev).

Responding to *Kaddish* brings blessing to the whole world

(*Siddur Shaar Yissoschar*). Whoever concentrates and answers "*Amen, Yehei Shemei Rabbah*" loudly and intently has all his sins forgiven, and shatters destructive decrees. By dint of one sincere "*Yehei Shemei Rabbah*", wandering souls who never did *teshuva* can rise to heaven, and the wicked get respite from *gehinnom*.

Rav Moshe Aharon Stern, Mashgiach of Kaminetz, was once invited to a very luxurious wedding in America. The door was open only to guests who showed their name cards to the doorman. Rabbi Stern had left his card behind, but he was unfazed. Surely he would be admitted just to go in and say mazal tov!

The gentleman at the door refused. All clarifications and justifications were to no avail. "No ticket, no entry," was the doorman's non-negotiable response.

"So it will be at the Heavenly court after 120 years," Rabbi Stern would tell his students. After spending its allotted time in gehinnom, the soul will be ready to move into his palace in Gan Eden. "Your ticket!" the guard will demand.

"What ticket?" the soul will wonder. "I have a palace in there that I painstakingly constructed with numerous mitzvos throughout my life. Please just let me in!"

But the guard at the gate will insist, "No ticket, no entry."

"Your palace awaits," Rabbi Stern would say, "but unless you present a ticket, you cannot get in. Where is your ticket? Your ticket lies within the simple word of 'amein'. Say amen with kavanah, and you have your ticket to Gan Eden" (HaMashgiach MeKaminetz).

A one million dollar check awaits you. All you have to do is pick it up. Would you walk or run? The reward for answering "*Amein, Yehei Shemei Rabbah*" is worth much more than that. We just have to be present in *shul* to avail ourselves of this grant (*Chofetz Chaim, A Daily Companion*).

Praying at Sunrise

"And this is the gateway to Heaven... and Yaakov arose early." (*Bereishis 28:17-18*). According to the *Baal HaTurim*, the juxtaposition of the two verses teaches that the Gates of Heaven open at daybreak. *Kevasikin*, the approximate moment of sunrise, is a very appropriate time for the morning prayer.

Davening at this first available opportunity provides benefits that last throughout the day. Feelings of happiness prevail for the one who makes the effort to pray at this early hour. He is protected from physical injury all day *(Berachos 9b)*. He enjoys fear of Heaven and is shielded from the accusations of the Satan *(Yerushalmi Berachos)*. And above all, he is assured a place in the World to Come.

Many great people of Yerushalayim davened kevasikin. The Maharsha Alfandri, who lived to about 118 years of age, davened at sunrise. Even when he was hospitalized, suffering excruciating pain all night, he still woke on time for the sunrise prayers.

Rav Chaim Yisroel Mordechai Harris always davened kevasikin in his neighborhood of Yemin Moshe. But on Rosh Hashana and Yom Kippur he walked to the nearest sunrise minyan in Batei Broida, a considerable distance away. On Yom Kippur he walked over the hot stones barefoot out of concern for the view of the Bach, who prohibits footwear of any material (HaChoma, Tammuz 5727).

For years, Rav Tzedakah Chutzin, head of the Iraqi community in Yerushalayim, regularly davened Shacharis with the first rays of sunrise. On a visit to Tel Aviv he asked his host where he could find a kevasikin minyan the next morning. "The nearest minyan is quite some distance away," the host replied apologetically. "I'm afraid it would take the Rav about an hour to get there."

"Don't be distressed," answered Rav Chutzin. "I'll just get up an hour earlier and make my way there."

It was still the wee hours of the morning when Rav Chutzin quietly slipped out of the house into the dark, empty streets of Tel Aviv. A short distance later, he glimpsed lights burning in a large building. He drew nearer to have a look. It was a beit knesset! Several men gathered around a table were learning.

Rav Chutzin entered. "Is by any chance a kevasikin minyan here?" he inquired. When he was answered in the affirmative, he exclaimed, "How wonderful! Apparently, the yetzer hara wanted to stop me from keeping my minhag, and made my host forget about your minyan close by. But once I started out, determined to walk even a full hour in order not to miss out on vasikin, the yetzer hara knew he had lost the battle. I just had to take the first step. Then Hashem led me here."

The Shul—Our Prayer Environment

History of the Shul

The *Bais Midrash* has been the central institution in Jewish life for centuries, a Jew's spiritual fortress amid hostile surroundings. In it he found inspiration and consolation, even as his existence was threatened. There the Jew communed with Hashem, found peace and solace studying Torah, and strengthened his faith to go on.

The *shul* was the community social welfare agency, where *tzedakah* was collected and dispersed, loans given and hospitality arranged. Meetings and gatherings were held there, since it was usually the only public building. It often housed the rabbinical court.

In its attempt to convert Jews, the medieval Church, aware of the *shul's* vital role in Jewish life, frequently tried to deny the right to build or worship in a synagogue, often restricting its height or visibility. Moslems also attempted to deprive the Jew of his place of worship.

In early communal prayer our ancestors gathered together and *davened* outdoors (*Tanis 16*). There was a special area set aside for prayer on the Temple Mount near the eastern gate. This was called the eastern street (*Divrei Hayamim 3:17*).

The first recorded indoor *shul* was the Hewn Chamber of the *Bais Hamikdash,* where the *Kohanim* would say *Shema* each morning (*Mishnah Tamid 3, 4 and 5*). This synagogue was built in the shape of a huge basilica (*Baraisa Yoma 25*). In *Yirmiyahu (39:8)* there is a reference to a *Bais Am*, which Rashi explains was a place where the people gathered to *daven.*

When the Jewish people were exiled after the destruction of the first *Bais Hamikdash,* they gathered to pray and read passages from the Torah. Traditionally, many would rise early and go to synagogue, following the exhortation of Yirmiyahu: "You will call on Me and go and pray to Me, and I will listen to you; you shall seek me out and discover Me when you seek with all your heart" (*Yirmiyahu 29:12-13*).

> *The prayers of Rav Meir of Amshinov were an outpouring of the soul. "How should I daven?" a young man once asked him.*
>
> *"Open the siddur and say each word loudly and distinctly, thinking what each word means," replied Rav*

Meir. "For example, 'Va'ani berov chasdecha avo beisecha—I enter Your House through Your chesed.' Who am I, a creature of flesh and blood, full of wrongdoings, to come before You? The answer is 'through Your chesed.' Only through Your great compassion am I allowed to enter shul and speak to You."

The prayer meeting was called *Knesses,* gathering. The place itself became a *Bais Knesses.* The Greek word synagogue has the same meaning. In Yiddish it is a *shul,* from the German *schule,* a school. As the synagogue was used for prayer as well as study, and to emphasize the dominance of study over prayer, the *shul* was called *schule* (*The Minhagim Rabbi Chill*).

In addition, the first letters of the Hebrew words "*shivchu ve'hodu li'shemo*—they praised and gave thanks to His Name," make up the word *shul.* The name implies that the synagogue is where the Jew offers his praise and thanksgiving to Hashem (*Ibid*).

Ancient Appearances

By the time the second *Bais Hamikdash* was destroyed there were a total of 480 *shuls* in Yerushalayim (*Kesuvos 105*). Each had an elementary school for basics and a high school, where *Gemara* was taught. Beitar had 400 *shuls* (*Gittin 58*). In Teveriya there were 13 shuls (*Berachos 8*).

There were *shuls* for different craftsmen. For example, coppersmiths had their own *shul (Megillah 26*). Babylonians, Romans and Alexandrians prayed in different *shuls* (*Megillah 26; Yerushalmi Yoma 7, 1; Yerushalmi Megilah 3, 1*).

Josephus mentions synagogues in Antioch (Syria), Greece, Rome, and different cities in North Africa. There were many synagogues in ancient Egypt. Descriptions of two have come down to us. The *Gemara* and *Tosefta* describe the great s*hul* of Alexandria (*Succah 4, 4; 5, 1*).

A Jew living in Alexandria during the period of the second *Bais Hamikdash* wrote about *Shabbos* in an Egyptian *shul*: "On the seventh day the Jews stop all work and proceed to the synagogues. There, arranged in rows according to their ages, the younger below the older, they sit quietly as befits the occasion, with attentive ears. Then one of them takes the books and reads aloud to the others..." (*Blessed is the Daughter, p.119*).

The *Gemara* in *Succah* describes the interior of a *knesses* in Alexandria: "He who has not seen the double colonnade of Alexandria in Egypt has never seen the glory of Israel." It was said to be like a huge basilica, one colonnade within the other, and to hold twice the number of people who went forth from Egypt. There were seventy-one cathedrals of gold, corresponding to the seventy-one members of the Great Sanhedrin—none of them containing less than twenty-one talents of gold. In the middle was a wooden platform where the synagogue beadle stood with a scarf in hand. When the time came to answer *amein*, he waved his scarf, and the congregation duly responded.

Seating was not random. Goldsmiths, silversmiths, blacksmiths, metalworkers and weavers sat separately, so a poor man entering the *Bais Knesses* could recognize the members of his craft. He could appeal to them and obtain a livelihood for himself and his family.

Sanctity of the Bais Hamikdash

Once the *Bais Hamikdash* was destroyed, the synagogue became the focus of the Jews' most intimate daily religious experience. In time it became a stand-in for the *Bais Hamikdash*. Because the *shul,* in effect, substitutes for the *Bais Hamikdash,* the worshiper should face the *Bais Hamikdash* irrespective of where he sits in *shul*.

Rabbi Eluzar HaKafir said that in the future all synagogues and houses of study will be adjoined in *Eretz Yisroel* (*Megillah 29*). The *Maharasha* uses the following verse to explain the *Gemara*: "I rejoiced when they said to me 'To the House of Hashem let us go.' Our feet stood within your gates, Yerushalayim, Yerushalayim which is built as a city that fosters togetherness" (*Tehillim 122:1-3*).

In these verses *David Hamelech* compares going to the synagogue to standing in the *Bais Hamikdash*. "Yerushalayim which is built" refers to the future, when the *Midrash* tells us the *Bais Hamikdash* will be as big as Yerushalayim, and Yerushalayim will be as large as the entire Land of Israel. Why will the *Bais Hamikdash* be so vast? The answer is alluded to in the verse itself: "fosters togetherness." In the future when Yerushalayim is rebuilt, all other "sanctuaries," the *shuls,* will be gathered together. All *shuls* that were established in exile will be adjoined to the designated place of Hashem, the *Bais Hamikdash.*

The *Michtav M'Eliyahu* (*vol. 4, p.130*) says this is true of any building that was elevated by being used in the service of Hashem. Primary examples are places designated for prayer and learning Torah. A shul is called a *mikdash me'at*—a diminutive sanctuary; the exhortation "and My Sanctuary you shall revere" (*Vayikra 19,30)* applies to every *shul* (*Mishnah Berurah 151,1).*

> *The Rebbe Reb Elimelch of Lizhensk, before entering the shul to pray, would say: "Know where you are entering, what you will do there, Who is in this house, Whose house it is, and Who empowered you to enter this house" (Nefesh Shimshon p. 35).*

The *shul's* appearance is vitally important. Woe to people who care for their own houses but neglect the house of Hashem, and happy is the community whose synagogue is its most prominent and attractive building. We do not decorate our *shuls*, however, so as not to be distracted from our prayers. Windows should be above eye level, so the sky is visible but not the distractions of the street. Every city whose roofs are higher than the synagogue will ultimately be destroyed, as it says in *Ezra 9:9*, "To exalt the house of our G-d and to repair the ruins of it." *(Shabbos 11).* [Implying that only when "the house of G-d" is exalted are the ruins repaired.]

The Proper Time

Everyone should try to arrive in *shul* on time, so that they are able to settle down before beginning to daven. We can then think of what our prayers should accomplish, reflecting on our needs and how Hashem can meet them. Those who come late are unable to *daven* properly, for they are rushed from the beginning.

> *In a private discussion about the importance of davening on time, the Nitra Rav mentioned a bochur who said he had come to davening early—during Pesukei De'zimra. The Rav exclaimed, "Is that called early? I'm not on such a high level spiritually, but I once came to davening in the middle of Birchas Ha'Shachar, and I felt so bad I couldn't calm down the whole day!" (Divrei Yona vol.1, p. 83)*

Hashem lends a hand (as it were) to those who make an effort to arrive on time. When Hashem sees they are truly sincere in their desire to be prompt, all obstacles disappear.

The Rav explained that the *yetzer hara* is allowed to employ various means to disrupt a person's service to Hashem. When the *yetzer hara* deals with someone determined to prevail at all costs, his mandate requires that he withdraw from the skirmish *(Tuvcha Yabiu I, p. 52).*

> *A Polish Jew living in a village wanted to arrive on time for davening, but his good intentions were never realized, as he had intestinal problems. One day he tried even harder to be in shul for the start of davening. He rose early, but while he did arrive earlier than usual, he missed the beginning of davening. Disheartened, he resolved to do better. Next morning he arrived in shul promptly for the first time. From then on, his problems disappeared.*

A person should never leave a *shul* as if trying to escape. He should be as a person taking leave of a king, preferring to spend more time in his presence (*Menoras Ha'Maor Light III, 3*). The early pious ones would spend an hour meditating after prayer, for they were not eager to end their *tête-à-tête* with Hashem (*Tur ch. 93, as cited by Tefillas Chanah*).

> *Reb Ber Nichamkin was a prosperous merchant from Homil. Though hard working, the Lubavitcher chosid somehow found ten minutes every morning to sit outside the shul after morning prayer. There he sat in silent contemplation.*

> *On a visit to Lubavitch, Rabbi Shalom Dov Ber Schneersohn noticed him sitting alone every morning and*

asked what he was doing.

The chassid replied, "This is all due to your grandfather, the Tzemach Tzedek. I once had a private audience with him, and he discussed self-refinement and the constant service of Hashem. 'People think this is reserved for scholars,' the Rebbe told me. 'Nothing could be further from the truth. Everyone must make demands on himself. Even businessmen need to ask themselves what they are up to. They must reflect on what they have done until today and what they intend to do in the future. A practical time for this is after prayer,' concluded the Tzemach Tzedek.

"I immediately applied what the Rebbe had advised," explained Reb Ber. "Every day after prayers I sit alone for ten minutes and examine my spiritual achievements. I decide what needs to be done and how to attain greater spiritual heights" (Sichos 5697).

A person leaving before *Kaddish* identifies himself as a scoffer. He devalues *amein* and *yehei shmei rabbah*. If he hurries to work, he is guaranteed not to succeed (*Yalozu Chassidim*).

A deceased pious man appeared to his friend in a dream and informed him that he was not permitted to enter the circle of tzaddikim because he left shul before Aleinu (Sefer Chassidim 155). A similar story is told of a righteous woman who was banished from the presence of the righteous ones because she had left before Kedusha (Ibid 779).

Respect for the Synagogue

Walking into a *shul* should be an experience that prepares a person for communing with his Maker. The laws of respect for a *shul* promote an atmosphere that engenders a worshipful, meditative mood. An awareness of the *shul's* distinction and an attitude of awe and respect generate an environment of spirituality.

It is customary for the worshiper entering *shul* to recite the verse, "How goodly are your tents O Jacob, your dwelling places, O Israel"*(Bamidbar 24:5)*, and then sit for a few moments to meditate. Before leaving the *shul,* he should again sit and meditate for a short while.

The *Gemara* in *Megillah (28a-28b)* lists numerous activities that may not be done in a *shul*, including behaving in a light-headed manner and spending purposeless time there. The *Rambam* (*Hilchos Tefillah, Perek 11 Halacha 6),* and the *Shulchan Aruch (Orach Chaim Siman 151 Seif 1),* include behaving with inappropriate jocularity and foolishness in this prohibition, as well as engaging in idle conversation. The *Sefer Chareidim (9:19)* notes that this prohibition is in force even when it is not *davening* time. He concludes by suggesting that one should learn in this regard from the behavior of non-Jews, who stay completely silent in their houses of worship.

If non-Jews treat their houses of prayer with respect, certainly we, who stand before the King of Kings, should do no less (Sefer

Mitzvos Ha'Katan, Mitzvah 11). Yet we bow our heads in shame when our prayer services are compared to those of the gentiles! All the news, the trivial happenings of the world, is shared in shul. There is so much laughter and frivolity; one would think the purpose of the gathering was social (Sulam Bais Kel).

The honor of the *shul* requires that it be kept clean. Some of our most respected Rabbis would tidy the *shul* themselves to emphasize its great holiness.

> *Rashi's rebbe, Rav Yaakov ben Yakar would clean his shul with his beard (Sefer HaChassidim). In Kelm, boys vied for the privilege of cleaning the Bais Midrash.*

To insure that the exalted status of the *shul* is maintained, the following rules must be observed:

Eating, drinking and sleeping in the *shul* are forbidden. Sauntering aimlessly or using the *shul* as a shortcut are forbidden. If one enters for some other purpose, such as calling a friend who is inside, one should first sit down briefly and recite some passages from the Torah (*Mishnah Torah Hilchos Tefilah II; Shulchan Aruch, Orach Chaim 150-154).*

One may not use the *shul* to take shelter from the heat or rain *(Megilah 27).*

It is forbidden to enter a *shul* with one's head uncovered.

In certain Oriental Jewish communities it is customary for the congregants to remove their shoes before entering the *shul.*

The bearing of weapons is forbidden, for a *shul* should bring peace, happiness and contentment. Weapons cause death *(Minhagim, Rabbi Chill).*

The *shul* should be erected on the highest ground in town, so a Jew can literally look up to his house of worship *(Shabbos 11).*

Rabbi Yehudah Tzadkah was careful not to eat anything in shul unless he required the nourishment to continue learning. He was once brought a cup of tea while learning. He had only drunk half when he closed his sefer and prepared to leave. "Why don't you finish your tea?" someone asked.

R' Yehudah replied, "I have finished studying for the moment. Before I was drinking so I could continue with my studies, but now that I am leaving, why should I drink?"

"Why don't you drink and then learn some more?" the Rosh Yeshiva was asked.

He ended the conversation by commenting that it was not appropriate to learn in order to drink. However, it is fitting to drink in order to learn (Ve'Zos Le'Yehudah).

Of Talking in Shul

One who speaks during prayer is guilty of *masig gevul,* stealing the sanctity of the *shul (Hilchos Teshuvah, 26).* One should avoid all unnecessary talking in *shul.* A person who comes to *shul* and talks to others is considered a sinner who causes others to sin; this behavior forfeits his portion in the World to Come *(Dover Shalom p. 70).*

> *A pious man once met Eliyahu the Prophet. He was loading three hundred camels with punishments. "Who are these for?" he asked. Eliyahu replied, "For one who talks between Baruch She'amar and the end of Shemoneh Esrei" (Orchos Yisroel citing the Pesiktah).*

Speaking in *shul* is contemptuous and arrogant behavior. "Woe to the one who chats idly in the *shul.* He proclaims his distance from Hashem. Regrettably, he lacks faith. Alas he has no part in the G-d of Israel. In chatting idly, he shows that as far as he is concerned, Hashem does not exist. He is not afraid of Him. He disgraces the higher purpose of the *shul" (Zohar, Trumah 13 1b).*

It is inappropriate to discuss even important *mitzvah* matters in *shul,* to avoid disturbing other people's meditations *(Or Hazafun).* The *Chidah* says the same of sharing Torah thoughts, and also adds that it sets the wrong precedent for those who are not learned *(Pesach Einaiyim).*

Rav Ezra Attiah used to pray in a synagogue near his house. When he concluded that he couldn't stop the persistent talking during prayers, he started praying elsewhere.

Once he sat in shul with two other Rabbis. While they waited for prayers to begin, the other two shared Torah thoughts. Rabbi Attiah advised them to wait until after prayers. "Others now entering shul will see you talking and conclude that you are simply conversing. And I, too, would like to hear what you have to say later" (Ha'Morah).

Someone who talks during prayer is called a wicked neighbor *(Rokeach 26)*. He publicly demonstrates that he does not believe in Divine Providence or in reward and punishment *(Shevet Mussar ch. 17)*. Even if he only winks his eyes or gestures with his hand, the Torah refers to him as "a man who does not call out to Hashem" *(Yeshayahu 43:22; Yoma 19)*.

The Zelach frequently lectured his congregants on the evils of talking in shul. At first, out of embarrassment, they kept silent when he looked their way. But with the passage of time, even a stern expression from the Rabbi did not help. He wrote, "They bring evil upon their souls, disturb their neighbors and indicate they have no part in the G-d of Israel. They are compared to Menashe, who set up an idol in the sanctuary. They created destructive forces that will demolish the shul, unless they repent" (Derushei Ha'Zelach 5356).

Rav Avrohom Sabo, one of the banished Spanish Jews of 1492, suggested that talking during *davening* and during the reading of the Torah caused the tragedy that befell Spanish Jewry *(Tzror Ha'maor).* The author of the *Shulchan Aruch* refers to the sin of those who speak of profane matters during the repetition of *Shemoneh Esrei* as "too great to bear." He does not refer to the desecration of *Shabbos* or eating on *Yom Kippur* in such stringent language!

This term is first used by Kayin, in referring to his sin of killing his brother Hevel. Rashi explains that Kayin meant to say, "You carry the upper and lower worlds, and You can't carry my sin?" Ultimately Hashem reached an understanding with Kayin, accepting his repentance and enabling him to remain alive. His sin thus became bearable. It is a horrifying to consider that speaking of profane matters during prayers is worse than killing a third of the world—a sin that remains too great to bear.

When a boy repeatedly spoke during davening, Rav Shraga Feivel Mendlowitz told him to leave. "Get out! When you are no longer in the yeshiva world, you can speak!"

On another occasion, Rav Shraga Feivel found himself praying with a minyan of businessmen who talked continually. After prayers were over, he admonished them with the words of the prophet Yirmiyahu (7:11): "Has this Temple, upon which My Name is proclaimed, become a cave of criminals in your eyes?" (Reb Shraga Feivel)

The years 1648-49 were filled with systematic barbaric torture and murder of the Jewish people at the hands of the Cossacks—a wave of suffering that would not be endured again until the Holocaust. It was revealed to Rabbi Yom Tov Heller, better known as the *Tosfos Yom Tov,* that the suffering of those years was a punishment for speaking during prayers. Rabbi Heller composed a special *Mi She'Berach* with singular blessings for those who refrain from conversing during *davening:*

> *"He Who blessed our forefathers—Avraham, Yitzchak and Yaakov, Moshe and Aharon, David and Shlomo—may He bless everyone who guards his mouth and tongue and refrains from talking during the prayer service. May the Holy One, Blessed is He, protect him from every trouble and distress, from every plague and illness; may all the blessings written in the Torah of Moshe and in the books of the Prophets and Writings be applied to him; may he merit seeing his children alive and established; may he raise them to Torah, the wedding canopy, and good deeds; may he serve Hashem our G-d in truth and integrity."*

The Shimloi Rav wrote that he had tried to prevent the Nazi bloodbath by begging his congregants not to speak in *shul,* especially during *davening (Lechem Shlomo).* The *Bais Yisroel* (in another version, *Baba Sali*) noted that Sephardic communities were mostly sheltered from the wrath of the Holocaust. He attributed their survival to their care in praying respectfully and not speaking during *davening (Matnas Chaim, p. 193).*

One troublesome issue must be addressed. Even if Jews did not pray with proper reverence prior to the Holocaust, certainly their attitude changed once the suffering began. Throughout Eastern Europe Jews gathered together, fasting and beseeching Hashem to annul the evil threatening them. Why didn't their prayers mitigate the harshness of the judgment?

This question is reinforced by our knowledge of prayer's power. The Torah tells us that Hashem promises He will respond when we call out to Him *(Vaeschanan 4:7)*. To reinforce this concept, our sages required that on Purim we read the *Megillah*, detailing the salvation of the Jews through prayer *(Rambam, end of introduction to Sefer Hamitzvos)*.

The solution to this dilemma can be found in *Malachi* (1:6-7):

"A man will honor his father and a servant his master. If I am a Father, where is My honor? If I am a Master, where is My fear? So says Hashem, master of Hosts, to you, the priests who dishonor My name."

"You asked, 'How have we dishonored Your name?'"

"Hashem replied, 'You offer loathsome bread on my altar.'"

"You asked, 'How have we repulsed you?'"

"Hashem countered, 'When you said the table of Hashem is loathsome.'"

Once the Jews belittled the Temple service, their sacrifices were no longer welcome. Prayer is subject to the same criteria. If we disparage our time with Hashem, the prayers we utter are not acknowledged. We essentially undermine the power of our prayers—both then, and in the future.

The weapon that had protected us through the ages could no longer protect us. When we called out to Hashem to annul the catastrophic decree against the Jews, He responded from Heaven, "If I am a Father, where is My honor? If I am a Master, where is My fear? So says Hashem, Master of Hosts, to you, the priests who dishonor My name."

Speaking of mundane matters during the *chazzan's* repetition of the prayers is certainly "a sin that can not be borne"! We ruin our relationship with the Master of the World and undermine our future prayers.

The *Mishnah Berurah (Ibid. Seif Katan 2)* treats at length the severity of the sin of talking in *shul*, considering it an act of belittling the honor of Hashem in His Holy place. Not just that—it will likely lead to *lashon hora* and arguments. One should therefore only speak words of Torah and *tefilah* in a *shul*. Elsewhere in the *Mishnah Berurah (Orach Chaim Siman 98, Seif Katan 3)*, he states that it is wrong for a parent to allow his child to talk nonsense in *shul*. It is noteworthy that the *Rema (Ibid Seif 1)* rules one should not kiss one's children in *shul*, to emphasize that there is no love like the love of Hashem.

The *Kaf HaChaim (ibid. Siman 151:8)* describes the severity of the sin of talking in *shul*: one who talks in *shul*, he declares, would be better off not coming at all. He also criticizes those who learn Torah and discuss it publicly during *davening*. He adds that one must be even more diligent on *Shabbos*.

The *Chayei Adam (Klal 17 Seif 6)* writes that the *mitzvah* to revere a *shul* is of Biblical origin, and states that one who talks in *shul* can be said to deny Hashem. The *Magen Avraham (ibid. Seif Katan 3)* notes that the holy *Ari* only said words of *Tefillah* in *shul*, avoiding even discussions of *mussar* and *teshuvah*, lest he be led to improper topics.

The *Mishnah Berurah (ibid. Siman 124 Seif Katan 28)* writes that we should educate our children to show respect in *shul*. He adds that it is better not to bring children who play in *shul*, until they can behave, for playful children disturb parents and other worshippers and they will acquire bad habits that will last a lifetime.

While it is not recommended, if one must talk, one should leave the *shul* in order to do so.

> *Rav Shmuel Aharon Yudelevitz always avoided speaking in shul, though he taught in a Bais Midrash, which was also used for davening. Once R' Avraham Yoffen visited the Yeshiva. After R' Shmuel Aharon finished his own lecture, R' Avraham gave a lecture and a mussar talk. When finished, he turned to R' Shmuel Aharon and began talking. R'*

Shmuel Aharon listened intently, nodding his head. R' Avraham continued talking as R' Shmuel Aharon walked him to the door of the Bais Midrash. As they stepped past the door, he responded to R' Avraham's comments. He had remained silent while inside the Bais Midrash.

The *tzaddik* of Bnei Brak, Rabbi Moshe Mandel, wrote, "I fail to understand how talking in *shul* became so widespread. Most people think there is nothing wrong with talking in *shul*. And since they're in the middle of a conversation, they miss out on saying *amein*. And I heard the Rov of Bistritz, R' Shlomo Zalman Ulman, say, 'Someone who does not answer *amein* will not rise at the Resurrection of the Dead' " (*Ha'Rav Mandel)*.

The *Rema (Shulchan Aruch Siman 124, Seif 7)* writes that young children should be trained to answer *amein*. Of course, the best way to properly teach one's children is by positive example.

A man and his son stood in shul praying. When the congregation answered amein, the son would utter all sorts of nonsense. The father ignored him. Those praying nearby told him to reprimand the child, but the man replied that he was only a child. This scenario repeated itself all the days of the holiday, and the father never reproved the child.

His punishment was severe. His wife, children and grandchild died—a total of 15 souls. Only two sons survived, one who was crippled and blind, the other foolish and wicked (Tanna Debei Eliyahu Rabbah 13, 8).

Rabbi Moshe Mandel said he could understand how a person came to steal, eat non-kosher food, even succumb to immorality, for man's physical desires take hold of him and lead to sin. These forces are difficult to overcome. But chatting in *shul* isn't a response to the body's craving; it is an expression of a person's will. Man resolves to sin, rebel against the *Ribono Shel Olom* and treat his *shul* with contempt *(Ha'Rav Mandel).*

We must recognize the results of not taking prayer seriously. The only way to repair the damage is to repent. We must confess, accepting responsibility for improving the quality of our prayers.

> *"For Hashem's sake, let us be quiet in the Beis Haknesses. Our reverent silence during tefillah will speak very loudly to Him Who holds our fate in His hands.*
>
> *Communicating with Hashem is our only recourse in this era of trial and tribulation. There is too much ugly noise in our world today. Let us find peace and tranquility while we stand before Hashem in prayer" (Selected Writings, Rabbi Shimon Schwab).*

When we are in *shul* we must exclude the outside world. Only then can we ensure that Hashem will take us under His wing and respond to our cries. We will thus be spared untold pain and merit the coming of *Mashiach* and the rebuilding of the *Bais Hamikdash (adapted from Matnas Chaim).*

A Designated Place

One who believes that his physical position is unimportant in prayer—for it is, after all, the spirit that counts—underestimates the body's significance. Designating a set location maximizes the body's contribution to our prayer (*Daas Torah*).

It is the awareness of the need to enhance one's prayer that makes the act of establishing a designated place so commendable. Rabbi Y. Z. Segal stressed setting aside a place for service of Hashem to show how much importance we attach to that service. Because it is so special, we will perform it only in a particular spot. It is not a burden, but a privilege.

We will not choose a location carelessly; praying in this space is part of our prayer ritual and is important to us (*Rif*). Making our way to the designated space shows we relish our prayer and wish to make the best of each exchange with Hashem (*Rif on Ein Yaakov Berachos 6*). This type of prayer is a serious charge, not a casual commitment (*Ha'Mussar Ve'Ha'Daas Bereishis 152*). A person who *davens* just anywhere, in contrast, suggests that prayer is a burden to be shed as quickly as possible.

An entity that occupies a set place is strong and deeply rooted. A tree that has been growing in one place for a long time, with firm roots, will not budge when a strong wind blows. A person who has a designated place for *tefillah* will similarly forge a very strong connection with Hashem over an extended period.

The *Maharal* explains that for *tefillah* to be absolute, it cannot be a casual act of worship. If *tefillah* is to achieve *deveikus*, a clinging to Hashem, it must be unswerving. If a person haphazardly *davens*, sometimes here and sometimes there, his *tefillah* will never attain *deveikus*.

By establishing a specific place for *davening* a person shows his prayers are dependable. It is therefore fitting, as the *Gemara (Berachos 7)* states, that "whoever establishes a place for *tefillah* will be saved from his enemies" *(Nesiv Ha'Avodah ch. 4)*.

> *Rav Nosson Wachtfogel warned that a person should never pray outside the main sanctuary. It is not respectful to pray in the hallway. A person who does so loses out on many of the benefits of prayer (Leket Reshimos).*

A Special Power

The designated place for prayers has a special power. The verse says that Avraham arose in the morning "to the place where he had stood" (*Bereishis 18:22*). The verse does not say he prayed, only that he returned to the place where he had prayed for Sedom and Amorah. This can be compared to a man who made a request of the king. After a few days he returns to the site where he made his appeal, so the king will see him and be reminded to fulfill his request. Indeed, Hashem remembered Avraham's request and arranged to save Lot (*Bais Elokim, Shar Ha'Tefillah ch. 5*).

The merit of Avraham comes to the aid of one who likewise designates a place for his prayers. His prayers will be answered, just as Avraham's were (*Bais Tefillah, Shaar Ha'Tefillah, ch. 5*).

A Rav visiting Vilna davened mincha in a small shul. As he began, he suddenly felt an extraordinary spiritual uplift. He was later told that this was the shul where the Vilna Gaon davened whenever he was in the city (Derech Sicha, p. 55).

Yitzchak also attached great importance to a set place for prayers. The verse says Yitzchak was coming back from *Be'er Lechai Ro'ee* when he met Rivkah and Eliezer returning from Aram Naharayim (*Bereishis 24:62*). The *Ramban* adds that apparently Yitzchak went there often. He had designated it as a place of prayer because it was there that Hagar's prayers were answered. Later we are told that Yitzchak settled in *Be'er Lechai Ro'ee (Ibid 25:11; Sforno ad. loc). Targum Yonasan* adds that Yitzchak was partial to this place because it was associated with Hashem's compassion for all His creatures.

Yaakov Avinu, too, made an effort to pray in the place sanctified by the prayers of his fathers. When he realized he had passed the spot where his father and grandfather had prayed, he returned to Mount Moriah to pray there *(Chulin 91).*

Daniel also knew the importance of a designated place. When Darius's advisers forbade praying to G-d, Daniel continued praying in his attic near an open window facing Yerushalayim. Three times a day he bowed, praying to Hashem as before

(Metzudas David on Daniel 6:11). He could have prayed secretly, in a more discreet location—but the attic was his designated place, and he was determined to continue his devotions there *(Binah Le'Itim Es Ha'Zamir Derush 1 on Tefillah)*.

> *A marvelous parable is cited in the writings of the Ari Ha'Kadosh to illustrate the importance of a set place for prayers:*
>
> *A king who wishes to capture a city by penetrating the wall surrounding it, will aim many flamethrowers at one spot, concentrating on a single location until the wall is breached. If he loses his focus—shooting the flamethrower at one spot, then another, and then a third—the wall will not be affected by these random measures.*
>
> *After the destruction of the Bais Hamikdash, many walls of iron now separate us from our Father in Heaven. Our prayers are our flamethrowers. If we always pray in one location, our prayers will eventually rupture these iron walls. But if one prays in different locations, he will never succeed in creating the slightest hole in the wall (Besamim Rosh in the Siddur Otzar Ha'Tefillos).*

The place where a person prays is sanctified by the presence of the *Shechinah*. Each time he prays there he benefits from the sanctity of his chosen spot (*Emes Le'Yaakov on Berachos 6*). There is merit in the accumulation of prayers in one place (*Sefas Emes on Berachos 6, 2*). The *Sefas Emes* notes that a set place for prayer is also important at home. Ideally, one should choose a spot where no one will interrupt him (*Sh'lah Maseches Tamid).*

R' Yosef Chaim of Baghdad sees the establishing of a set place as alluding to orienting our hearts to Hashem. A person who only occasionally focuses on his prayers has not succeeded in establishing a fixed place. Only one who has a secure area in his heart for his devotions will merit the blessings intended for a fixed place *(Ben Yehoyada).*

> *When counseling bridegrooms on the basics of marriage, Rav Yaakov Kaminetsky would advise, "Instead of praying one day here and one day there, you should choose one shul and acquire a permanent seat. One of the benefits you'll reap is the friendship you'll develop with your fellow congregants. If you constantly change places, where will you make friends who will come to your son's Shalom Zochor or celebrate his bar mitzvah with you?"*

The Right Environment

Bais Hillel says that every action a man does influences him within and affects his environment without. The disciples of the *Baal Shem Tov* cite the story of two sages strolling through a field. Suddenly, one was almost overcome by an urge to kill his friend. How could a great sage contemplate murder?

The answer lies in the place where they were walking. This

field was the actual location where Cain had killed Hevel. This action—the first murder since the creation of man—was absorbed by the place, causing the sage to act against his nature and contemplate murder.

Likewise, a place used in a positive manner becomes a setting for furthering spiritual growth. This is why Yaakov returned to Mount Moriah to pray, where his ancestors had prayed, because *davening* there would enable him to absorb the holiness they had planted with their prayers.

If trees and stones can absorb holiness, how much more can a person's heart absorb it? A single effective prayer encourages your heart to pursue a second high-quality prayer (*Introduction to Tefillas Channah, p. 39).*

When a person *davens* in *shul,* his prayers strengthen and encourage those around him. Unfortunately, the reverse is also true—a prayer environment filled with levity and carelessness pulls down everyone within it. A person should therefore always pick a *shul* with serious congregants who will support his prayer. The *shul* environment then becomes a springboard for first-rate prayers. If he falters, he will be invigorated and uplifted.

A person should always choose a spot conducive to praying correctly. If he sits next to frivolous people, it will be difficult for him to pray as he should. He will gain much if he sits among those who pray earnestly, with devotion *(Derech Hachaim 71).*

He should avoid those who use the synagogue as a place to catch up on the latest news and gossip *(Chofetz Chaim 9, 64).*

Leading the Prayers

Historically a *shaliach tzibbur* was needed because prayers were not written down, and many people did not know them by heart. Prayers were led by someone well versed in the text. Others would repeat after him, or listen and respond with *amein* at the end of a *beracha.* The *Gemara* outlines the procedure for inviting someone to conduct prayers, whether the person asked should initially appear reluctant, and under what conditions he should immediately accept the offer (*Berachos 34b*).

A professional *chazzan* should not hesitate when asked to lead prayers, while a neophyte should always hesitate. Rashi hints at this in the verse, "*Kerav el ha'mizbeach*—come close to the altar." Rashi adds, "*Lomah atah bosh, ke lecha nivcharta*—why do you hesitate, you have been selected for this?" (*Rashi on Shemos 9:7; Panim Yafos, in the name of his uncle's daughter*).

Originally the *chazzan* served as *shamash,* charged with keeping order in the *shul* (*Yoma* 7,1). In larger *shuls* the *chazzan* became the regular, paid *Shaliach Tzibbur,* with smaller *shuls* hiring a *chazzan* only for *Yom Tov.*

The leader of the prayers serves as an emissary for the congregation. A strenuous effort should be made to find prayer leaders who are eloquent, G-d fearing Torah scholars, capable of inspiring worshipers to reach a higher level of prayer. If the congregation reveres its prayer leader, it will be easier for him to bring them to a higher level of worship.

The *Yom Kippur* prayer, "*Hineni he'ani mima'as*—behold I am poor in worthy deeds," perhaps more than any other prayer, highlights the responsibility of a *Shaliach Tzibbur* as an emissary of the congregation.

The *Gemara* describes a suitable *shaliach tzibbur* for a public fast day: "One having a large family but who has no means of support, who draws his subsistence from the field, and whose house is empty, whose youth is unblemished, who is meek and acceptable to the people; who is skilled in chanting, has a pleasant voice, and possesses a thorough knowledge of the Torah, the Prophets and the Writings, of *Halacha* and the *Aggadic Midrash* and all the Benedictions" (*Taanis* 16a).

With many children and no sustenance, he will be moved to pray with all his heart.

The *Baal Ha'Tanya* refers to damage caused by those incapable of leading prayer but insist on doing so: "That office is abandoned to whoever wishes to stride forth and seize the honor, or because no one even desires it." People should be selected to lead. "Men who worship word by word, out loud, neither overly prolonging the prayers nor racing intemperately, G-d forbid, theirs is the duty to lead the prayers, each on his day as determined by the congregation. This is amplified in ancient amendments in many cities. I come not to renew them, but to strengthen and invigorate them, never again to be weakened, G-d forbid" (*Kuntres Acharon Essay 9*).

A Chabad chassid acting as a mentor for the young chassidim of Vitebsk was the regular prayer leader for their minyan. Their prayers were uttered purposefully, unhurriedly, with great concentration.

When their mentor visited the Maharash before Rosh Hashanah, he was asked, together with the other chassidim, "Where are you holding?" The Rebbe thus expressed in interest in how they had progressed since their last meeting.

The mentor answered, "I am acting as baal tefilah, prayer leader."

The Rebbe responded, "A baal tefillah stands on the brink. If he is worthy, he achieves merit and brings merit to others. If he is unworthy, he sins and brings others to sin."

The chassid later commented, "The Rebbe reached into my heart and endowed me with a new soul."

When he returned to Vitebsk and led the prayers for kabbolas Shabbos, crowds gathered in an attempt to discover why this normally quiet minyan was now praying with the enthusiasm usually present at Kol Nidrei (Sefer Ha'Yechidus pp. 163-164).

When R' Avraham Pester and his children led the prayers, the Chassidishe shul in Batei Ungarin would fill completely, with people overflowing into the courtyards nearby. Like the early pious ones, his morning prayers would last until past noon.

His son R' Yaakov inspired awe. When R' Yaakov prayed, people would forget their hunger. It was as if they experienced the service of the Kohen Gadol in the Temple. R' Yaakov's face took on an otherworldly look when he prayed, making him unrecognizable. He had but to utter the first words of the selichos prayer, and crying would start. Sometimes he would have to wait for the sobs to subside so he could continue with the prayers.

"R' Avraham and his children buttress the city of Jerusalem," said Rav Yosef Chaim Sonnenfeld.

When the Satmar Rebbe visited Yerushalayim for the holy days and heard R' Yaakov praying, he said, "The inconveniences of the trip were worthwhile just to hear his prayer." When he passed away, Rav Dovid Jungreis ordered that the tombstone be inscribed with the words, "His prayers inspired the masses to teshuva."

When R' Yaakov's son R' Itche began leading the prayers, he asked his father for the key to success. "Say the prayer of R' Elimelech with devotion before you pray. If it is impossible to do so, repeat to yourself, 'I will place Hashem before my eyes always,' and 'I will always remember before Whom I stand: before the King of Kings, the Holy One Blessed be he.'" R' Yaakov himself would always murmur those words as he went up to lead the prayers.

When R' Itche prayed on Rosh Hashanah, everyone was moved to tears. The entire city turned out to hear at least part of his prayers. The "Hashem, Hashem" of the Neilah prayer was awesome (Sipurim Yerushalayim).

Reb Shraga Feivel Mendlowitz personally chose the baalei tefilah in the Mesivta, even on weekdays, since a good chazzan has the ability to arouse the emotions of the congregation. To qualify as a chazzan in Mesivta, one had to pronounce the words correctly, possess a clear and melodious voice, and daven with feeling (Reb Shraga Feivel, p. 140).

Rav Shmuel Dovid Ungar became the son-in-law of his Rosh Yeshiva and uncle, Rav Noach Baruch Fisher. Shortly before the chuppa, Rav Fisher gave Rav Noach Baruch a heartfelt blessing—and then added a strange request.

"Whenever you are asked to be a shaliach tzibbur," he told Rav Shmuel Dovid, "make sure you never turn down the

offer."

Rav Noach Baruch's students thought there might be some deep secret behind this request and begged him to reveal it. "My motivation was very simple," he replied. "Rav Shmuel Dovid's prayers are so heartfelt that I am sure everyone listening to him will be inspired with the love of Hashem. Why should he deprive anyone of such an opportunity?"

Rabbi Tzedakah Chotzin established his own private shul at the outskirts of the Geula neighborhood, calling it Shemesh Tzedaka. Morning prayers were at sunrise. Only a chazzan he approved of could lead the prayers. He selected pious individuals who were meticulous in their mitzvah observance. Praying alongside the chazzan, Rav Tzedaka would say each word as if he was counting diamonds (Oros Mi'Mizrach).

The Chazzan's Repetition

Talking is forbidden during the *chazzan's* repetition of *davening*. One must pay full attention so he can answer *amein* properly *(Mishnah Berurah, Siman 56)*.

One should not learn or recite other prayers during this time *(Shulchan Aruch Siman 124 Seif 4; Mishnah Berurah Seif Katan*

17). If those studying Torah turn to their texts, less-focused individuals will likewise not listen to the *shaliach tzibbur* and engage in idle talk, Heaven forbid. This will cause many people to sin *(Mishnah Berurah 124).*

During *Kaddish,* even meditating on Torah thoughts is forbidden. One has to focus on saying *amein* in the proper fashion as discussed in the *Shulchan Aruch (Orchos Yosher).*

> *After his death, a certain pious man appeared in a dream to another pious man, sporting a large stain on his forehead. He had not been careful to avoid speaking during Kaddish (Sefer Ha'Chassidim as cited in Mishnah Berurah 268).*

If there are not nine people concentrating on the *shaliach tzibbur's* recitation of the blessings, the blessings can be said to be in vain, writes the *Shulchan Aruch (124,4).* Talking during *chazaras hashatz* can cause this to happen.

"Whoever speaks in *shul* during the time the congregation is busy with the praise of Hashem shows that he has no portion in the G-d of Israel" *(Shulchan Aruch HaRav 124).* Rav Shlomo Zalman Auerbach equates speaking during *Chazaras Hashatz* to sitting in the Temple of the King and humiliating His Name *(Keser Meluchah, page 402).*

In contrast, one who acquires the habit of listening attentively to the *chazzan's* repetition of *Shemoneh Esrei* will acquire many virtues. He will master the ability to concentrate, learn to be dutiful, and gain the capability of controlling his impulses *(Or Yechezkel, Reshimos Talmidim).*

Chazaras hashatz is even more significant than the silent *Shemoneh Esrei* because it fulfills the directive of the *Gemara*: "If one sees that his prayers are not answered, he should repeat the *tefillah*." According to the Vilna Gaon, this refers to *chazaras hashatz (Shearim Be'Tefillah p. 14).*

> *Sefer Ha'Chassidim tells the story of a chassid who appeared to his friend after death. His friend was horrified at the green appearance of the departed soul. The soul explained that his face was disfigured because he had spoken during the chazzan's recitation of Vayechulu, Magen Avos, and Yisgadal.*
>
> *Rav Shlomo Zalman Auerbach was always completely focused on the words of the chazzan. He followed every word and would often approach the chazzan after davening to thank him for his pleasant rendition. He would warn others of the obligation to listen carefully to each word and respond amein after each beracha.*
>
> *When his students asked if they could learn during the chazzan's repetition of Shemoneh Esrei if there was a minyan to respond amein, he would openly rebuke them. "Are we so careful about wasting a minute that we feel comfortable taking this time as well?"*

Rav Yosef Dayan prayed so slowly that he always missed the chazzan's repetition of the Amidah prayer. He would therefore rush to join another minyan which was just beginning the repetition of the Amidah. Often he would start the Shacharis prayer in the Ohel Rochel synagogue and complete his prayers in the Nahar Shalom synagogue.

Motzai Shabbos he would daven in one synagogue and then got to the Ohel Rochel synagogue, where prayers ended later, since a shiur continued past the time Shabbos officially ended. He would enter as the chazzan started the blessing "Ve'Atah Kadosh" and join in kedusha.

The gabbai's attention was drawn to the newcomer who uttered his prayers in a loud, strong voice. Not knowing the Rav's stature, he rebuked him for always coming late. One of Rav Yosef's disciples asked the Rav why he didn't enlighten them. Rav Yosef always responded, "Don't tell them. I prefer the criticism" (Od Yosef Chai, p. 144).

The Power of Blessing

A Daily Reminder

Blessings accompany us through the day and carry the benefits of prayer into our daily activities. Focusing our enjoyment of nature, guiding our pleasures and our performance of *mitzvos*, constantly reminding us of Hashem's presence and our mutual relationship: our *berachos* declare that Hashem is everywhere, and His influence pervades our world.

The *berachos* we say throughout the day were instituted to remind us of our indebtedness to Him. When we say a blessing properly, we acknowledge that we have not forgotten Hashem (*Olas Tamid*). It is best to say *berachos* aloud since this inspires us to focus and concentrate with more attention (Shulchan Aruch, siman 61:4). Blessings uttered in this manner reinforce and deepen our intimacy with Hashem.

Rabbi Shimshon Dovid Pincus took a full hour to count the Omer every day of the sefirah, and twenty minutes to recite the blessings over the Chanukah candles. He recited the beracha of Asher Yatzar with special fervor, and in many of his lectures he urged listeners to realize the importance of this tefillah.

"We spend a third of our lives sleeping," he would say. "If a person has the correct intention when reciting the Krias Shema prayer before sleep, his sleep becomes an important part of his service to Hashem."

A World of Enjoyment

Hashem made a world filled with beauty, giving us senses to perceive these wonders and the ability to appreciate them. Blessings help us take the time to observe Hashem's gifts. They ensure that we are aware of the marvels of this world and rejoice in it properly. A thoughtful *beracha* heightens our enjoyment throughout the day.

Blessings are a joyful acknowledgment of Hashem's kindness. Hashem does not need our *berachos*, but we do. They help us take pleasure in what we have and remind us of our good fortune. We feel exuberant and enjoy life more by being conscious and appreciative of all we are blessed with. Blessings ensure that we do not forget that it is our Creator who provides our needs.

A grandchild once watched Rabbi Avigdor Miller eat an apple. He began by examining the apple closely. "Ribbono Shel Olam," he exclaimed, "look at this magnificent apple You created! The wisdom in its waterproof enclosure, the beauty of the deep, tantalizing red color, and the temptingly delicious aroma with which it is perfumed. How can I even begin to thank You for the tree it grew on? And to think that You made it all for me!"

Only then did he enunciate the beracha clearly, as if the Ribbono Shel Olam Himself were sitting before him (Jewish Observer, Rabbi Shmuel Brog).

Counterattack

When satiated, man tends to forget his Creator. The physical act of eating leads to a type of intoxication, which propels our G-d consciousness to the back burner. As man sows and reaps, kneads and bakes, toiling until he has bread to eat, he may come to believe that his success is a result of his own efforts.

To counteract this tendency within man, we were commanded to bless Hashem before each meal and to mention Him again after every meal thus quashing these thoughts (*Yalkut Yitzchak, quoting Oros Ha'Mitzvah; Meshech Chochma*). One who eats a meal without concluding with sincere heartfelt thanks to the Creator, owner and supplier, is not merely a thief, but is frustrating the entire purpose of the meal, which is to bring people to the great accomplishment and happiness of becoming more aware of and acknowledging the Creator (Sing, You Righteous, Rabbi Avigdor Miller, pg. 352).

Rav Shimshon Raphael Hirsch notes that *berachos* elevate man spiritually. A blessing said with proper intent and concentration affirms Hashem's rule and recognizes the source of life's gifts. When saying a blessing, we should remember we are speaking directly to Hashem, dedicating ourselves to His service, and acknowledging that whatever power we have acquired must be used to serve Him.

Blessing for the World

When we remember all good comes from Hashem, and only He can provide our needs, we earn that blessing. A *beracha's* acknowledgment allows us to receive Hashem's goodness and secures further blessing (*Mitzvah 430; Nefesh Ha'Chayim)*. When we make a *beracha* thus inviting Hashem into our lives, Hashem responds by generating worldly abundance (*Rabbeinu Bachya*).

Each type of food has its own way of bringing its blessing to the world. When we ascertain the correct *beracha* on each food, we provide a conduit for the blessing of that food to come down to earth. One who eats without a *beracha* brings about a loss of that type of benefit and so diminishes the bounty to the public.

Chazal in *Berachos* tell us that R' Chanina said, "If someone enjoys anything of this world without a *beracha*, it is like stealing from Hashem and from *Knesses Yisrael*- the Jewish people." The *Gemara* adds that he is considered "a comrade of a destructive man" (*Mishlei 28:24*)—a reference to Yerovam ben Nevat, who degraded Israel before their Father in Heaven. Not only did he sin, but he influenced others to sin. A person who eats without a *beracha* similarly despoils others by his actions, for he diminishes the blessing and bounty to the world.

Before eating, R' Dovid of Lelov would pray for three things. He would request that he achieve all necessary spiritual rectifications with his food; he would ask that the food contribute to his health and wellbeing; and he would call upon Hashem to ensure that the food be absolutely kosher (Niflaos Chadashos Likutei Divrei Dovid).

Spiritual Sustenance

Acknowledging Hashem adds a spiritual dimension to eating. Showing gratitude indicates a refined character, and each *beracha* we say aids in this refining process.

The Ben Ish Chai quotes a Rav who suggests that the *man* the Jews ate in the wilderness was spiritual food, requiring no elevation, and therefore no *beracha*. Rav Yosef Chaim rejects this approach—for there still remained the need to show one's gratitude, adequate reason to say a *beracha*.

A chassid once wondered if there really was a significant distinction between him and his Rebbe. Both were mortal, and both said blessings before eating.

The chassid arrived at the Rebbe's tish, still pondering this dilemma. The Rebbe, who had already begun his discourse, began to speak about the differences between a Rebbe and a chassid.

"The chassid says a blessing so he can eat," the Rebbe explained. "The Rebbe eats so he has the opportunity to say a blessing" (Rav Aharon Ha'gadol of Karlin).

A person must be careful that his *berachos* do not demonstrate his craving for food. One who hastily says the blessing so he can wolf down his food is punished with premature death (*Yesod Yosef 87, citing Sefer Hachassidim 46*).

The Power of Concentration

A person who does not concentrate on a blessing's meaning reveals insensitivity and a disregard of Hashem's mastery of the world. A blessing without *kavanah* is simply an empty shell (*Mishnah Berurah 5, 1; Chayei Adam 5, 26*).

The *Chida* writes that the letters of the word *Bereishis* represent, "*Be'kol ram avarech shem Hashem tamid*—in a loud voice I will bless Hashem always." Saying blessings aloud improves our concentration (*Shulchan Aruch 61, 4*).

Rabbi Ben Zion Abba Shaul calculated that a person says about two and a half million blessings in seventy years. But when he stands before the heavenly court after his time in this world, he may find only hundreds of *berachos* to his credit. What happened to the trainloads of blessings he had uttered? Only a small percentage—the equivalent of a few small bags—was said with proper piety, joy and devotion (*Tuvcha Yabiu I, p. 270*).

A prominent Rabbi once fainted. While unconscious, he suddenly found himself witnessing the proceedings in the Heavenly Court as the soul of a great person was being judged.

The man was presented with a sefer Torah. "Did you observe everything written in the Torah?"

"Yes," he replied.

Swarms of angels created by his good deeds immediately appeared to confirm the truth of his word.

A copy of the Arba Turim, a code of Jewish law, was brought next. "Did you observe the Oral Law?"

"Yes," he replied.

Additional angels joined the first group to testify on his behalf.

"Were you careful to always pronounce the name of Hashem with kavanah?"

The man remained silent.

"Were you careful to always pronounce the name of Hashem with kavanah?" they asked again.

Again he said nothing.

Destructive angels suddenly appeared, created by all the blessings he had said without kavanah. One by one, each announced the event which had brought them into existence.

The heavenly court turned its wrath on the poor soul. He was given a choice—Gehinom or reincarnation. He chose Gehinom (Le'Shichno Tidrishu).

It is important to concentrate when pronouncing Hashem's name in the *berachos*. It is therefore forbidden to recite a blessing while busy with other matters (*Shulchan Aruch 183, 12; Mishnah Berurah 191, 5*). The *Shaar Zion* explains that this is why we do not shake the *lulav* when we say Hashem's name.

The brother of the Sh'lah HaKodesh stressed the importance of stopping to consider what one is about to say before beginning a blessing. Take a moment to gather your inward emotion and make it part of the beracha (Comments to Yesh Nochalin).

Before we make a beracha on bread, Rabbi Yisroel Miller asks us to picture ourselves as guests at the Creator's table, and to consider how miraculous it is that bread originates from the earth (What's Wrong With Being Happy).

Using a text aids in *kavanah.* It helps us focus on the content of the blessing.

Rav Chaim Ozer Grodzinsky of Vilna was blessed with a phenomenal memory. He acknowledged that he was unfamiliar with the concept of forgetfulness. One example underscores his tremendous talent:

As rabbi of the city, Rav Chaim Ozer was responsible for all Free Loan Societies. He kept detailed records of all transactions in a thick notebook. Once after the family moved, they discovered the book was missing. The family was distraught, as there was no other record of loans outstanding and payments received.

When Rav Chaim Ozer saw his family's distress, he sat down and wrote the entire book from memory, including names, dates and amounts. Ultimately, the book was discovered, compared with the list compiled from memory—and they were found to be identical.

Even so, Rav Chaim Ozer never said the Grace after Meals

by heart. He always used a text (Birchas Hamazon Kinyan Torah, p. 3).

Rav Shach always carried a bentcher in his pocket. He was sitting in a succah when he noticed some words in the bentcher had been erased by repeated use. He rose and went inside to find a siddur before proceeding further (Ibid p. 4).

It is well known that the Tosher Rebbe always says berachos from a text.

Saying blessings with proper intent destroys negative forces which would otherwise attach themselves to one who does not say blessings properly (*Derech Emunah citing Shaar Hagilgulim II*). The blessing elevates earthly food, purifying it prior to consumption (*Knesses Yechezkel Bereishis).*

The Belzer Rebbetzin once heard a chassid saying a beracha hurriedly, without concentrating. Deeply troubled by the piteous blessing, she went over to the chassid.

"Let us make a simple reckoning together," she suggested. "The cookie you are now eating is made from wheat. When the wheat was growing in the field, it prayed to Hashem that

it continue to grow and thrive. Hashem had the angel appointed over the wheat promote its growth.

"When it was fully grown, the wheat desired nothing more than to reach the hands of a Jew who would say a blessing on it, so it prayed that it not be among those kernels that fell in the field. When it was finally ground, it begged Hashem that it not be discarded with the chaff. When it joined the flour in the sack, it prayed that a Jew say a proper blessing that would bring pleasure to its Creator.

"Are all those prayers valueless in your eyes? Don't those pleas affect you and inspire you to say your blessing properly?" the Rebbetzin asked (Tuvcha Yabiu).

The Text of Blessings

The blessings we say were established by Ezra and his court (*Rambam, Hilchos Berachos* 1, 5), with the *Anshei Knesses Hagedola* formulating the precise wording.

The first word, *Boruch,* should be translated as "source of blessing."

"The blessing with which one blesses the Master of the world, brings blessing to the heavens and earth. He who blesses the Master of the Universe is blessed. He who does not bless the Master of the Universe is not blessed" (*Zohar, Vayechi*).

According to *Chassidic* teaching, the word *Boruch* literally means "drawing down". Everything in life—health, prosperity, joy, wisdom, peace of mind—needs to be drawn down from its potential, spiritual state into the actuality of our physical existence. Spiritually, it all exists: we are all healthy, wealthy and wise. The problems we experience in life are basically a matter of something wrong in the wiring. We're not connecting; our spiritual and physical selves are having trouble communicating. A blessing makes the connection into reality.

The next word in the blessing is *atah*, You. We have the tremendous privilege of calling G-d "You", as we would when speaking to a person right in front of us. This is a great expression of Hashem's love and mercy toward all creatures (*Avodas Yisroel, Lech Lecha*).

The Blessing of *Shehakol*

When we say *shehakol* we acknowledge Hashem as the Creator of all enjoyable gifts in this world, dedicating ourselves with enjoyment to His service.

> *Rav Yisrael Salanter was indebted to the owner of a restaurant for providing an insight on the nature of shehakol. He had questioned the owner about the high price of a cup of tea—which was, after all, just a cup of hot water with a few tea leaves and a spoonful of sugar.*

"It is true that tea leaves and sugar can be purchased for a couple of pennies," the owner told him. "But when the tea is served in a restaurant, other charges are included. You pay for the décor, music in the background, waiters in uniform, and a delicate china cup. All this costs money."

Rav Yisroel was delighted with the explanation, for it enhanced his understanding of the shehakol blessing. "In the past when I recited this blessing, I intended to thank Hashem for the water He created. But now I realize that the blessing also includes thanks for the fresh air we breathe while drinking the water. It includes thanks for the beautiful world around us, including the music of the birds and the splendid colors of the sky and grass and flowers. We must thank Hashem for all this and more when drinking our water!" (Simcha, the Spark of Life)

A disciple of R' Moshe of Kobrin was consumed with various worries, and decided to travel to Kobrin to see his Rebbe. He went directly to the Rebbe as soon as he arrived. At exactly that moment, the Rebbe was served something to eat.

The Rebbe saw the chassid, but did not greet him; instead he recited the blessing, "Shehakol nihiyey bidevaro," and ate.

When the Rebbe finished eating, he saw that the chassid was still standing there. He called out, "I thought you resembled your father, but I see I was mistaken.

"Your father once came to see me, bearing a heavy load of worries. He also came in when I was saying shehakol. After the beracha I asked him if he had something to ask me.

"'No,' your father said, and added nothing more. And do you know why? When he heard the words, 'that all was created by His Word,' all his questions were answered. If a person believes that everything is done by Hashem's Word, why should he worry?"

The Rebbe extended his hand in parting to the chassid, who returned home, once again calm and trusting.

A Rav from Tunis was attacked by an Arab who tied him up, intending to kill him. The Rabbi's two students begged him to leave the rabbi alone, but the Arab warned them if they said another word he'd kill them first.

The Rav urgently whispered to his students to run for their lives. As the Arab prepared his knife, he told the Rav that he was ready to fulfill his last wish. The Rav asked for a cup of water. When the Rav received the cup of water, he said the beracha shehakol in a loud, strong voice.

The instant he finished the beracha, an Arab sheik passed by and called out, "Kill all the Jews, but don't touch their rabbis!" The Arab had no choice but to drop his sword and free the Rav.

Later the Rav explained to his students that he had asked for the water for he knew that by saying the blessing shehakol with deep concentration, evil decrees can be annulled (Our Heroes, C. Walder).

During World War II the Nazis rounded up a large group of Jews, intending to shoot them. One righteous individual asked his son to get him a glass of water. When he had the water, he began to shout the blessing in a voice like thunder. The moment he ended the blessing, they suddenly heard explosions—the Russians had arrived! The Germans fled and the Jews were saved.

The son asked his father how he had succeeded in saving them. "The text of the Gemara guided me. It says, 'If one says shehakol nihiyeh bedivaro over anything, you are yotzei (fulfill your halachic obligation).' The word for 'anything' can also refer to 'any problem,' and 'yotzei' can be translated as 'be rescued.' All salvation is hidden within the words of shehakol."

Someone came to Rav Yehudah Zadka and asked him to pray for his sick child. Rav Yehudah calmed the distraught father and then handed him a candy. He said, "Let us first say the blessing shehakol nihiyeh bedivaro, to sweeten the harshness of the decree." Then he said a mi sheberach for the child and wished the father well.

The father returned to the hospital and was told his child had improved dramatically. In a short time he had recovered fully and was released (Ve'Zos Le'Yehudah).

Birchas Hamazon

After we have eaten, we are commanded to bless Hashem our G-d for the good land He has given us (*Devarim 8:10*).

Why do we thank Hashem for the land every time we eat? Would we thank a friend for the beautiful furniture in his dining room after he invited us for a meal?

Consider the following scenario. A man is lost in the desert, far from civilization. He is overcome by hunger and thirst, with no place to shelter from the fierce sun. Suddenly a helicopter appears. It quickly settles to the ground, and the pilot brings out a table, a chair, all types of food and drink. "Look at everything we brought, especially for you," he says. "Eat and enjoy!"

Would expressing thanks for the food be adequate? Think of

all the details of this elaborate arrangement—it would be appropriate to thank the pilot for every single one!

Hashem is constantly renewing our existence. Each meal is celebrated by a renewed creation in a renewed environment. It is therefore appropriate to thank Hashem for every single detail—the land *and* the food (*Hegyonei Mussar III p. 212*).

When we say *Birchas Hamazon,* we not only thank the farmer who plants the wheat, and the one who bakes the bread—we thank all of those who are involved in preparing our food: from the wife of the farmer who cooks meals for her husband, enabling him to work, to the grocer, the trucker, the suppliers, and the factory workers. Without all these individuals being sustained by Hashem, the bread would not reach our table.

In essence, *Birchas Hamazon* is our thanks to the G-d who sustains us.

Before reciting Birchas Hamazon, pause for a moment and think of all the different foods you have eaten during the course of the meal. Someone who eats in a restaurant examines the bill carefully to determine that the charges are correct. It is likewise appropriate for us to itemize the different foods for which we must thank Hashem (Notrei Amen).

Why are we given food? So we have the opportunity to thank Hashem. In a similar vein, it is because we require *tefilah* that Hashem causes rain to be dependent on our prayers (*Tefillah Ve'Lev, Rav Elimelech Bar Shaul*).

Bentching with Devotion

Some *mitzvos* have *mazel*, the Yaavetz writes. The *mitzvos* of Purim, burning of *chometz,* differentiating between dairy and meat—all are fulfilled carefully and attentively. Yet there are *mitzvos* without *mazel*—such as *bentching*. While everyone enthusiastically complies with the "eating until satiety" component, the "blessing Hashem your G-d" part is fulfilled quietly and halfheartedly. Words are said without devotion, often not even pronounced properly. Clearly it is one of the *mitzvos* that have no *mazel*! (*Chasdei Hashem*).

It is time we made an effort to reverse that trend. We are thanking Hashem for all He provides us; we are expressing our gratitude for the strength which is restored to us as we eat. Surely this merits excitement and sincerity! One who focuses on the words of *bentching* will merit hearing this blessing sung by King David, at the festive meal prepared by Hashem for the righteous in the World to Come (*Yesod Yosef* 87). Let us take the four, five or six minutes to focus exclusively on the words we are saying.

> *The Maggid of Mezritch warned his followers to be more careful with bentching than with prayer. For prayer is of rabbinical origin, while bentching is a Biblical obligation (Toldos Aharon Shoftim).*

Rav Chaim Palagi saw *Birchas Hamazon* as a way to achieve long life. It is also a means of diverting Hashem's anger (*Rav*

Shach). Others note that *Birchas Hamazon* has no letter *pei*, signifying that one who recites this blessing with devotion will be spared *af*, *shezef*, and *ketzef*—anger, violence and wrath, all of which end with the letter *pei* (*Ateres Zekeinim Shulchan Aruch Orach Chaim 175*).

> *A man once appeared to a relative more than a year after his death and informed him that he was still being punished for not having said Blessings and Birchas Hamazon with proper devotion. The relative wondered at the extended punishment, as Gehinom only lasts for twelve months. The soul informed him that the sufferings he was enduring of late were of a lesser degree than those he had endured within twelve months of his death (Chayei Adam 5).*

Hashem provides trouble-free *parnassa* for those who are careful to say *Birchas Hamazon* with devotion (*Chida*). The Kotzker Rebbe demonstrates that *Birchas Hamazon* is an ancient means of acquiring fear of G-d—for when *Avrohom Avinu* wished to lead the masses to acknowledge the existence of Hashem, he would advise them, "Bless Him Who has provided for you."

When we are about to *bentch,* it is not unusual for the doorbell and the phone to start ringing. The *yetzer hara* knows the importance of *bentching* and therefore arranges many distractions (*Tuvcha Yabiu, Vol. I, p. 230*). Blessed is the family that makes an effort not to speak in the same room where someone is *bentching*.

The author of *Yesod Ve'Shoresh Ha'Avodah* would pray that he not be disturbed while *bentching*. "My Creator! Have compassion on me. Please make sure that no one should call on me during my *Birchas Hamazon*, so my *kavanah* is not disrupted" (*Tzavaas Yesod Ve'Shoresh Ha'Avodah 10*).

A young Torah scholar visited a public library in Israel to consult a rare text he could not find elsewhere. He brought along a sandwich from home, since there was no kosher restaurant in the area. When he got hungry, he found a place to wash and sat down to eat.

After finishing his lunch he began bentching with his usual enthusiasm. The head librarian apparently was listening to the words he carefully enunciated aloud, for when he finished, she approached with a question.

"You seem to add two additional words when you recite the blessing. You said 'velo nikashel—that we not stumble' after 'shelo neivosh velo nikalem—that we not feel inner shame nor be humiliated.'"

The young man was surprised by this question from the seemingly irreligious librarian. She explained that she had came from a very religious home, but had abandoned Judaism over the last few years.

"These words are part of the bentching, though not every text contains them," he explained. He promised he would

send her proof of his assertion.

The young man searched through his home and went through numerous siddurim in various shuls, but could not find a source for the wording. Finally, in the Meah Shearim neighborhood, he discovered an old haggada with the words "velo nikashel."

He copied the page and circled the words in red, then surrounded the circle with red arrows—making it impossible to miss. He did not know her name, so he sent it to the library with a note that it should be given to the head librarian. He then promptly forgot about the matter.

Many months later the young man received an ornate wedding invitation. He quickly concluded that he knew neither the chassan nor the kallah. But since he had another wedding to attend on that night, he decided to drop by the unknown wedding. Perhaps he would discover why he had been invited.

It didn't take long after his arrival at the wedding to conclude that the families were completely unknown to him. "The invitation must have been a mistake," he told his wife, and they turned to go.

"Excuse me," a man approached them. "Can you give me your name?"

The young man identified himself.

"Please don't leave yet," the man requested. "The kallah would like to speak to you."

The young man was astonished, but he naturally agreed.

He approached the kallah. "Do you recognize me?" she asked.

The young man shook his head.

"You are the most important person at this wedding!" she declared.

"What do you mean?" the confused young man asked.

"I am the head librarian who had the argument with you about Birchas Hamazon. It is thanks to you that I became a baalas teshuva, and I am now establishing a Torah home."

Sensing his disbelief, she continued, "I am ashamed to admit that at the time that we met, I was contemplating marrying a non-Jew. Though I was no longer observant, my conscience was still bothering me, and I hesitated to go ahead with the wedding. My fiancée finally gave me an ultimatum—either agree to go ahead with the wedding by a certain date, or our relationship would be terminated.

"The day arrived. I was still in a quandary. I went to work

and found a letter on my desk. Because you did not know my name, it had taken weeks for the letter to reach me. I opened it and two words circled in red jumped out at me: 'that we not stumble.'

"I was completely shaken. I suddenly perceived what a dreadful step I had been contemplating. It was clear to me that I could not go ahead with the wedding.

"I told my fiancée that our relationship was over. One good deed led to the next—I became religious once again, and I have now married a Torah-true Jew with the willingness to establish a committed Jewish home." (Be'Tuvcha Yabiu II p. 265).

The Text of Birchas Hamazon

Birchas Hamazon is comprised of four blessings. Moshe formulated the first, expressing gratitude for the *man* in the desert. Yehoshua originated the second, praising Hashem for allowing the Jews to enter into and dwell in the land of Israel. King David and King Shlomo formulated the third blessing, praising Hashem for Yerushalayim and the *Bais Hamikdash*. (After the destruction, this blessing was adjusted to refer to the rebuilding of the *Bais Hamikdash*.) Rabban Gamliel wrote the fourth blessing, praising Hashem for the miracle at Beitar, when He preserved the bodies of the Jews who were slaughtered by the Romans (*Berachos 48b*).

"Who sustains the world." After we enjoy our food, we acknowledge Hashem as the sustainer of our existence. We dedicate to His service the power and strength we have gained from His gifts. The *Zohar* stresses the importance of saying *Birchas Hamazon* with special joy, expressing our gratitude for His kindness (*Shaarei Kedusha 1, 6*).

In earlier times it was clear that our food was sent from Hashem. Man's flour came from wheat grown in his own field, which he had cultivated and harvested. What he spread on his bread was available courtesy of his cows or orchards. He might go to his garden to pick cucumbers and tomatoes as the final touches to a tasty meal.

Today we buy everything at a grocery store. It is much more difficult to locate Hashem behind the entire process. It is so much easier to get food—we forget who supports us. Stop for a moment when the meal is done, and think of the true source of the food you consumed.

Hashem provides our food *be'chen,* with an extra measure of grace. Many of our fruits and vegetables come in colorful, convenient packaging. Rabbi Yechezkel Avramsky would note how the orange is covered by a substantial peel, while inside, the delectable fruit is easily divided into sections. Others point to the apple, grape, and carrot, whose beautiful colors augment the enjoyment of our foods.

Hashem has also provided us with tremendous bounty.

Quantities of various foods are readily available. While we may justifiably argue that since Hashem created us, He is required to provide for us, the tremendous varieties of foods exceed this obligation (*Rav Shimon Sofer*).

When informed that a hospitalized Torah scholar needed a blood transfusion, Rabbi Avramsky sighed. He said he prayed every day that he should not become sick and require a blood transfusion, with the words, "Please make us not needful, Hashem our G-d, of the gifts of human hands." (Birchas Hamazon). "Though these words do not refer to a blood transfusion," he explained, " it is possible to add layers of meanings to all our prayers" (Pninei Rav Yechezkel).

The Pnei Menachem ate his meal hurriedly. But when he said Grace after Meals, he would firmly grasp the cup and enunciate the words slowly and carefully. When he reached the words "and on the great and awesome house upon which Your name rests," he would pause, and a sigh would ensue, rising from the depths of a broken heart.

He noted that when the Rebbe of Kotzk reached the words about rebuilding the Bais Hamikdash, he appeared to be in deep mourning (Pnei Menachem).

Some say *Amen* after each *Harachaman* in *bentching*. These requests are not an intrinsic part of *bentching*. They are requests that we pray will be granted in the merit of the performing the *mitzvah* of *bentching*.

Borei Nefashos

Hashem causes us to hunger and thirst as a means of elevating the souls within our food and drink. This is suggested by the words of the blessing *Borei Nefashos*. We thank Hashem for having created souls with deficiencies: "*Borei nefashos rabos ve'chesronan*." We can then consume and thereby elevate the souls within our food: "*Le'hachayos bahem nefesh kol chai*" *(Bais Asher Lech Lecha)*.

When the Bobover Rebbe, Reb Shlomo, prepared to say the blessing "Borei nefashos rabbos—Who creates many souls" at the home of a host who was childless, a guest who was also childless asked if he could be included in the blessing. The Rebbe replied, "The beracha refers to many souls, so it can include many different people." Within a year, both had been blessed with children (Retold by the Bobover Rebbe's nephew).

The Jewish community of the village of Kafania near Szighet supported themselves by selling whiskey. Wishing to deprive the Jews of their sustenance, the local priest influenced the people not to buy whiskey. When they realized their predicament, the Jews quickly sent a messenger to the Yitav Lev of Szighet, asking him to save their livelihood.

The Rebbe said, "We can interpret the blessing Borei Nefashos as follows. 'Hashem created many souls with needs'—such as the desire for drink. This gives sustenance to our brethren. If they do not provide that sustenance, then there is no need for those souls."

Shortly afterwards a plague broke out in the village of Kafania. The local landowner investigated and concluded that the people had taken ill as a result of parasites which infested their bodies. Drinking whiskey would have cleansed their bodies and raised their resistance to these parasites. Further inquiry traced the people's avoidance of whiskey to the priest's decree. The priest was imprisoned, accused of negligent homicide and severely punished (Gedolas Yehoshua II 66).

Tefillas Haderech

Saying the prayer for a safe journey with *kavanah* is the most effective way of ensuring safe travel from point A to point B.

Rav Elchonon Wasserman took a boat from France to England. R' Aharon Goodman, one of the leaders of Agudas

Yisrael, was on the same boat. The ship was overtaken by a ferocious storm, hurled about by the stormy waves. The passengers suffered intensely.

When they arrived in England, Mr. Goodman noticed Rav Elchanan disembarking and joyously ran to greet him. "How was the Rebbe's trip?" he asked with trepidation, quickly adding, "We were all deathly ill from the storm."

"I did not suffer at all," Rav Elchonon responded. "In fact, it was a pleasant trip. Perhaps you did not say Tefillas Haderech with the proper kavanah."

R' Elye Lopian was travelling from Yerushalayim to Haifa by train. Someone asked him if one should say Tefillas Haderech, the traveler's prayer. "Of course," he replied.

At one point he went to the restroom. After washing his hands, he motioned to a policeman to gather his colleagues. He told them he would say a blessing, and they should all answer Amen.

R' Elye said the Asher Yatzar blessing as he always did: aloud, word by word, with great emotion. They all answered Amen. He then said Tefillas Haderech.

A few moments later the train stopped, and remained in place for about half an hour. The passengers were told that a bomb had been discovered on the train tracks. Miraculously, it had not exploded.

R' Elye simply commented, "You see how important it is to say Tefilas Haderech" (Reb Elye).

Asher Yatzar

The blessing of *Asher Yatzar* is recited each morning as part of the *Birchas HaShachar.* It is also recited after relieving oneself. It affirms that Hashem is the One Who sustains physical life and expresses thanks to Hashem for all the wonders of the human body and for our over-all physical health.

We recognize that our bodies are complex and sophisticated systems. If one part of the system goes wrong, the whole body is affected. We therefore express our gratitude to Hashem that our bodies continue to function properly.

If one says this *beracha* with proper intent, his fear of G-d is reinforced (*Devarim 10:20, Olas Tamid*).

Rabbi Shalom Eliezer of Ratzferd, son of the Sanzer Rav, had a broken table that he treasured. How did it come to pass?

His elder brother, the Shinover Rav, once came for a visit. Rav Sholom treated his older brother with great reverence—

after all, the Shinever Rav was old enough to be his grandfather.

At one point, the Shinever Rav used the facilities. When he returned to the house, he began to say Asher Yatzar. Toward the end his voice faded; all assumed he had completed the blessing, and was now deep in thought. They waited respectfully for him to complete his meditation.

After several minutes, his fist came crashing down on the table, splitting the top, as he uttered the final words of the blessing: "Rofeh chol bassar u'maflih la'asos!"

Rabbi Shalom Eliezer would never permit his Rebbetzin to repair the table. Every time he saw it he was reminded of the proper way to recite this blessing.

The *Chofetz Chaim* and other great sages taught that saying *Asher Yatzar* with proper intent from a text has the power to ensure a healthy body and keep the doctor at bay. There are many people who were saved from severe illness by saying this blessing.

A worried Jew once came to the Chazon Ish in Bnei Brak. When the man entered he found the Chazon Ish saying the Asher Yatzar blessing, pronouncing each word slowly and clearly.

The man couldn't contain himself. He blurted out, "My

child has polio, and the doctors say there's no hope."

The Chazon Ish emphasized the last words of the blessing, "Who heals all flesh and acts wondrously." He then turned to the man and said, "So, you hear that Hashem does wonders."

Nothing more was said. The child had a completely recovery.

A son of a Kollel scholar studying in Bnai Brak was diagnosed with a terrible illness. The Kollel members undertook to say the blessing Asher Yatzar with intense commitment. The results were immediate—the sickness disappeared (Tuvcha Yabiu I, p. 269).

The Text of Asher Yatzar

"Who formed man with intelligence." The human body is extraordinarily sophisticated. It is truly amazing that we are able to ingest foreign material and process it to provide the body with the energy and materials it needs to continue functioning.

"Many openings and many hollow spaces." "Openings" refers to openings in the human body, such as the mouth, the nose, and the ears. "Hollow spaces" refers to hollow organs, such as the stomach, the intestines, and the heart.

The seat of Hashem's honor is mentioned here to teach us that Hashem concerns Himself with every aspect of our lives. He watches and knows everything (*Gra Imrei Noam ad loc.*).

"If one of these would be opened, or if one of these would be sealed, it would be impossible to survive and to stand before You." We have many openings that open and close, such as the heart, esophagus, and intestines. If they were to open at the wrong time, or if they were blocked when they should be open—life could not exist. At birth, all the fetal openings close, and all openings needed for life in this world instantly open (*Shulchan Aruch Orach Chaim 6).*

"Who works wondrously." This refers to the intricate system through which nutrients are separated from the food we eat and delivered to each part of the body. The undesired matter is then expelled, employing separate systems for liquid and solid wastes.

> *A young man studying in Rabbi Silberstein's Kollel would say Asher Yatzar in a loud voice, with great devotion. His recitation disturbed the others, who were forced to pause in their studies until he had finished. His fellow Kollel scholars wanted to know if they could ask him to say the beracha quietly.*
>
> *Rabbi Silberstein cited the response of the authors of the*

Responsa Min Ha'Shamayim comparing the blessing of Asher Yatzar to the blessing of Gomel, which is said when a person survives a dangerous experience. Consider how many miracles occur each time the body eliminates waste—certainly one would want to let others know that this "journey" had been successful!

Therefore, said the Rav, just as one says Hagomel with a minyan to publicize the miracle he experienced, it is acceptable to involve others in the blessing of Asher Yatzar.

The body resembles a balloon—an entity filled with air. But while a balloon deflates immediately if punctured, the human body with its many openings continues to function without interruption (*Berachos 60 Rashi*).

Forty-year-old Diane was an unaffiliated Jew when she first moved to Atlanta from New York. Slowly she began attending Shabbos services at a local synagogue. She came to realize that something had been lacking in her life; she began attending classes, in particular the monthly Torah From Dixie lectures. Month after month, she attended the classes and continued her growth as a Jew.

About a year after Diane began attending classes, her rabbi was at the grocery store, buying refreshments for a Torah From Dixie class that night. He bumped into a local rabbi, who asked why he was buying so much food. Upon learning of the upcoming class, the rabbi remarked that he had received an extra-large shipment of Asher Yatzar posters in the mail, which he was willing to offer the class participants. Diane's rabbi brought several posters to the class, and Diane took one home with her.

The rabbi received a phone call from Diane several months later.

She began by telling him how she had taken one of those posters home after a Torah From Dixie class. "I had never heard of the Asher Yatzar prayer before," she explained. "I hung up the poster that night and recited the prayer for the first time."

Diane had had a serious digestive problem all her adult life. She had gone to many doctors in New York and Atlanta, but no one could figure out what was wrong.

That night, after reciting Asher Yatzar for the first time, her problem miraculously disappeared. More than a year later, Diane's digestive problem has not recurred.

100 Blessings Daily

King David instituted the requirement to say 100 blessings daily, to stop a plague that was decimating the people. This plague continues to threaten in every generation. It can only be forestalled through carefully maintaining the practice of reciting

100 *berachos* every day (*Tur Orach Chaim 46*).

The hundred *berachos* protect against the hundred curses in *Parsha Ki Savo*. This includes the 98 curses that are explicitly written, as well as the generic, "every illness and every blow" (*Rokeach, Berachos 320*). Knowing the protective power of blessings should inspire us to recite the blessings with care and devotion.

There is a significant connection between the one hundred sockets that were used in the Mishkan and the one hundred blessings that a Jew is required to recite every day. Just as the sockets formed the foundation upon which the Mishkan rested, so the daily one hundred blessings form the foundation upon which the life of a Jew rests.

The word "adan—socket" is similar to the word "adon—master". By reciting one hundred blessings each day, a Jew declares that Hashem is the Master of the entire universe (Chidushei Harim, as cited in Maayanah shel Torah).

The Power of Tehillim

Praise Amid Affliction

Why are *Tehillim* (Psalms) so powerful? What lies behind their greatness?

The songs of King David were composed in stressful situations. Yet with every misfortune King David sang praises to Hashem—words of thanksgiving, words of repentance. He infused his experiences into the holy words of *Tehillim* and presented them to his people.

> *Nevuchadnetzer, king of Bavel, becoming aware of Hashem's wonders, wanted to sing His praises—songs finer than those of King David. But an angel struck his mouth, and his songs weren't sung (Sanhedrin 92b). The Rebbe of Kotzk explained that evil Nevuchadnetzer wished to sing while rich and comfortable, king of the known world. King David sang*

praises at every misfortune, even in pain. An angel hit Nevuchadnetzer, as if to say, "Now that you are in discomfort—will you still sing praises to Hashem?" (Sefer Lahavos Kodesh quoted in Meoros Daf Yomi Publication, Vol. 185)

King David knew that the source of all events, good or bad, is Hashem. In darkest times he would lift his eyes to Heaven and pray that Hashem save him. Amid his travails David recognized that deliverance was near: "I thank You, for You have afflicted me, and You have been my deliverance" *(Metsudah Tehillim, Sfas Emes).*

After salvation had arrived King David sang songs of praise and thanks. "I lift my eyes to the mountains. From where will my salvation come? My salvation comes from Hashem, Who created the heavens and the Earth" *(Tehillim 130).*

In all history there was none so afflicted as David Hamelech. Despised by his father, who thought him haughty; rejected by his brothers; pursued by his father-in-law, Shaul Hamelech, as well as his own sons—Avshalom sought to kill him, and Adoniyahu tried to ascend his father's throne. David constantly ran from one enemy to another, knowing no rest. All seventy years of David's life were filled with troubles and hardships (*Midrash Shocher Tov, Ishei Ha'Tanach).*

David epitomizes humility, total subordination to the will of Hashem, overcoming all adversaries with wisdom, calm and restraint. When David fled for his life from his son Avshalom, Shimi ben Gera cursed David, pelting him with stones. David's general Yoav ben Zeruah wanted to kill Shimi for his effrontery. David refused: "Let him be. Let him curse, for Hashem has told him to" *(Samuel II 16:11).* In the face of impudence David is silent. He attributes Shimi's insolence to Hashem's will, accepting it lovingly.

Through unwavering faith in G-d, David triumphed over all adversity. The Book of Psalms teaches us to be like King David, trusting in Hashem completely. "I had faith (even) when I said, 'I suffer greatly'" *(Tehillim 116).*

Yosef Chivan, *rebbe* of the Chassid Yaavetz, said, "If not for *sefer Tehillim*, we would be unable to praise Hashem properly." The title of a *sefer* of praises should have been *tehillos*. David Ha'Melech called the collection *Tehillim,* explains Rav Shimshon Raphael Hirsch, to indicate that they are incomplete. It is up to us to take these verses and verbalize them thus converting them to vehicles of praise for Hashem *(Introduction to Rav Hirsch on Tehillim page 12).*

For All Time

David Hamelech wrote for all Jews, for all times *(Midrash Tehillim 18).* The Psalms embody the universal experiences of life *(Malbim, Introduction to Tehillim).*

In *Tehillim* David joined the tribulations of his people to his own. When he petitioned for himself, he petitioned for the entire nation, for he identified with their suffering and joy (*Yalkut Me'am Loez, Preface to Tehillim*). He prayed for all our necessities, until the coming of *Mashiach*.

The deepest emotions of the human heart were expressed via King David's words. In joy or sorrow, triumph or failure, there is a chapter of *Tehillim* to fit the occasion *(Meor Ve'Shemesh, in the name of Radak)*.

The *Sh'lah Ha'Kadosh* felt *Tehillim* was the best means of achieving closeness to Hashem *(Hilchos Teshuvah, Inyanei Tefilla.)* Through generations, men have used verses of *Tehillim* to communicate effectively with Hashem. Many recite *Tehillim* daily. Some soothe the misery in their hearts. Others praise their Creator, expressing happiness and joy at their good fortune.

> *Reb Moshe Feinstein would say Tehillim each morning. For many years he spent his summer vacation at a hotel. There he could be seen saying Tehillim every morning at six o'clock. Other guests would gather to observe his Tehillim sessions. One of the guests was quick to say that it was worth coming to the hotel just to see Reb Moshe say Tehillim with such devotion (Siach Yisrael).*

The Chofetz Chayim once told his students the following story:

It was the custom in Galician shuls to recite Tehillim together late Shabbos afternoon until it was time to daven maariv of motzaei Shabbos. Once a Jew entered late Shabbos afternoon and noticed a friend alone in a corner fervently reciting Tehillim. He watched as his friend poured out his heart.

Swept up in the swelling emotion, he joined in. Soon the two men were reciting one chapter after another with great passion, as the tears rolled down their cheeks.

The sun set and it was time for maariv. The two men joined the maariv minyan. After davening, the man turned to his friend and asked that he share with him the burden that induced such heartbroken Tehillim.

The man explained that he had a wonderful daughter who had long since come of age. She was blessed with a good head and a heart of gold. "Such yiras shomayim! Her cooking is delicious, and she knows how to sew beautifully."

"So why isn't she married?" asked his friend in surprise.

"Because we have no money for a dowry," he replied. "All week long I am away, so I don't see her pain. But on Shabbos when I am at home, it eats away at me to see her growing older each day, with no hope of establishing her own home. It's too depressing to stay at home, so I come to shul and plead with Hashem to have compassion."

His friend was very touched. "You may find this hard to believe, but I have a son who is a yorei shomayim and has good midos. He also needs a shidduch, but I don't have the money to marry him off. You don't have money, and I don't have money. Let's make a shidduch between your daughter and my son."

On the spot they agreed to explore matters further. The match worked, and the couple had four sons, each a Torah scholar of note. One was Rabbi Yehudah Ha'Cohen, author of Kuntres Hasefeikos. Another was Rabbi Chaim Ha'Cohen. A third was Rabbi Mordechai Ha'Cohen, rav of Chodrov, and the fourth was Rabbi Aryeh Leib Ha'Cohen Heller, author of several seforim including Sheiv Shematisa, Avnei Meluim and Ketzon Hashulchan. All in the merit of Tehillim (Yated Ne'eman, A Point to Ponder, M. Rosenzweig).

There was once a righteous woman who recited Tehillim for women in labor, to ease their pain. No sooner had she begun reading the psalms than a healthy baby would be born.

The woman and her husband decided to move to Eretz Yisroel and settled in Tzefas. They agreed to conceal her special powers so she would not be called on constantly, thus hampering her immersion in prayer.

One day they heard of a suffering woman in the throes of labor. When the doctor declared the woman's life to be in danger, the woman felt compelled to help. She went to the woman's house and began saying Tehillim. As before, the baby was born shortly after. The residents of Tzefas realized that the Rebbetzin had helped the woman, and her reputation spread. Again she was called when a woman experienced difficulties in childbirth.

At that time Eretz Yisrael was ruled by Turkey. One day a sheik's daughter was having a difficult labor, and her doctor feared for her life. The sheik's adviser had heard that the Rebbetzin could help people by reciting Tehillim. Thinking she would fail, he told the sheik, who sent an urgent message to the Rebbetzin, demanding help for his daughter. She hesitated, but her husband insisted she go lest she endanger the Jewish community. Again her fervent prayers worked, and the sheik's daughter gave birth speedily and without complication.

The sheik was grateful and told the Rebbetzin, "Tell me your wish. I will grant it!" She shunned financial reward and told the sheik she wanted to recite the book of Tehillim in Me'aras HaMachpeilah—the cave, then off-limits to Jews, where our forefathers and mothers are buried, along with Adam and Chavah.

The sheik gladly consented, impressed by her modest request. Seeing the favorable impression the Rebbetzin had made on the sheik, the adviser decided to have her killed. He bribed the guard in the Me'aras HaMachpelah to lock the door of the chamber and trap the Rebbetzin, leaving her to die of hunger.

The Rebbetzin came to the holy site and began to recite Tehillim. The guard locked the door. After a few hours she completed her tearful prayers. But when she tried to leave, she found she was trapped.

She immediately grasped the evil scheme that had been planned. Taking out her book of Psalms once again, she prayed, "Hashem, if it is Your wish that I must die now, I accept this wholeheartedly. But I beg of You, please, I do not want to defile this holy place by dying here. Please, Master of the World, let me out so I may die elsewhere."

She continued her heartfelt plea until she fell asleep. She dreamt that a man of saintly appearance, a crown on his head, stood over her. "I am David Ha'Melech. Because you dedicated your life to reciting the Tehillim I wrote, I have come to save you." In her dream he led her out of the cave. When she woke, she found herself outside the Me'aras Ha'Machpelah (Gut Voch).

Protection and Salvation

The Talmud says one who studies the words of a sage forms

a bond with that sage. Even in the grave, the lips of that sage move as his teachings are uttered. King David himself stands beside one who wraps himself in the words of *Tehillim*. Reciting *Tehillim* protects those who utter the holy words, as well as their families and all Jews. It brings blessing and success *(Peleh Yoetz).*

Throughout generations—in all times, under all circumstances—*Tehillim* has served as the voice of the Jewish people. In it the Jew found comfort in the darkness of his troubles, and in it he saw a guiding light *(Me'am Loez Preface to Sefer Tehillim).* Many stories testify to the efficacy of the holy words of King David in bringing salvation.

One night Rav Yaakov Finkelstein was woken by a slight noise at his window. Opening it, he saw the Chazon Ish, who told him, "A young girl's life is hanging by a thread. The doctors have given up. It would be a good idea to gather a group of Bnai Torah and say Tehillim." Rav Yaakov quickly gathered some boys, and they said Tehillim with great devotion (Pe'er Ha'dor).

When one of R' Moshe Feinstein's grandchildren was ill, the news was kept quiet so as not to worry him. The situation worsened, and the child was rushed to the hospital. R' Moshe was then informed so he could daven on the child's behalf.

"Why wasn't I told?" he asked in anguish. He took his Tehillim, stood by the window and began to cry, tears streaming down his cheeks.

A few minutes later the phone rang. R' Moshe lifted his eyes from the Tehillim. "Are they calling from the hospital?" On receiving a negative, he lowered his eyes and continued saying Tehillim. This happened a few times.

Finally the hospital called. Rebbetzin Feinstein called from the kitchen, "They are calling from the hospital. He got a new medicine, and he is responding well."

"Baruch Hashem! Baruch Hashem!" R'Moshe called out. He closed his Tehillim. Sweat poured down his brow. He made his way slowly to his bedroom, where he collapsed on the bed and fell into a deep sleep (Reb Moshe).

Many years ago, a simple G-d fearing Jew lived in an Arab city. He had an Arab neighbor who always needed money, and he pressured the Jew to lend him a sizeable sum. The Jew felt compelled to lend the money, but stated the sum must be paid in full by a certain date.

When the loan was due the Jew came to the Arab for payment. The Arab put off repayment and told the Jew to leave.

One Friday the Jew appeared at the Arab's house, demanding immediate payment. The Arab asked the Jew to sit and wait for him to bring the money. The Jew sat patiently and began reciting Tehillim. When the Arab saw the Jew praying, he became enraged and decided to kill him.

The Jew, a G-d fearing man, kept saying Tehillim. From time to time, he came to the verse, "Free me, Hashem, from the evil man, from the violent man preserve me" (Tehillim 140:2). When he said this verse, it seemed to repeat itself! The Jew understood this to mean danger was approaching. He left and hid outside.

As the Jew left by one door, the Arab's brother, tired and weary, entered through another. He sat down on the chair the Jew had just left, resting from his travels. Suddenly the borrower came charging into the room, sword drawn, and attacked the man in the chair. When the Arab saw that he was not the Jew, but his own brother, he fainted in shock. The Jew saw this from his hiding place and escaped before the Arab could recover (Sefer Gedolas David).

A Rosh Yeshivah came upon Rav Shach saying Tehillim one morning. The Rosh Yeshivah explained that he had been saying Tehillim for many years, since visiting the grave of a scholar who performed miracles by dint of fervent Tehillim he said every day. Usually Rav Shach finished his quota early in the day, but that morning he recited it later than usual (Orchos Chasidecha).

Rav Shlomo Zalman Auerbach related the following story about his father, Rav Chaim Leib:

Late one night a woman came to my father, crying that her daughter was having a very difficult labor. She told my father that the doctors feared for her life and said that without performing a caesarean section the daughter could die.

"Should they go ahead with the surgery?" she asked. "Please pray for the safety of my daughter and her baby!"

Seeing the woman's deep fear and pain, my father in his great mercy began to console her, reassuring her that everything would be fine, and they should not perform the surgery. "Have faith in the Ribono Shel Olam, and your daughter and her baby will be all right," he said.

The mother was pleased to hear Rav Chaim Leib's response. She quickly thanked him and ran from the room to return to the hospital and tell the doctors not to perform the surgery.

As soon as she left, my father began to regret his advice. His first reaction had been to calm the woman and comfort her. Now he thought, "How could I say that if the doctors said the situation was life threatening? I was so concerned about making her feel better that I did not consider the dangers involved."

My father tried to catch up to her to tell her she should follow the doctor's orders. But the woman was already far away and could not be found.

My father returned home brokenhearted, worrying about the safety of that mother in labor. He instructed everyone in our house to stay up all night saying Tehillim. I have never seen my father as downcast as he was that evening. He cried all night, praying for the delivery to go safely.

The next morning the woman returned tears of joy in her eyes. "Thank you, Rebbe!" she cried. "Thanks to your blessings and encouragement, my daughter gave birth to a healthy baby, and everyone is doing well!" (Retold by a student of Rav Shlomo Zalman)

Rebbetzin Chaya Mushke, wife of the Tzemach Tzedek of Lubavitch, used to say Tehillim regularly. Before traveling to a conference to defend Torah Judaism the Tzemach Tzedek instructed his sons to say Tehillim with their mother every day, including Shabbos, so he would succeed. Later the Rebbe told one of his sons, "My success in Petersburg was mainly due to the chapters of Tehillim your mother said." (Diary of Reb Yosef Yitzchak Schneersohn, Lubavitcher Rebbe).

In Times of Distress

For centuries, pious Jews have turned to *Tehillim* for solace and encouragement when times were difficult. They instinctively felt how it speaks to the heart of every man and woman at all times. Every dispirited heart in need of salvation or relief from pain finds a salve in the words of *Tehillim (Sefer Hamidos Shaar Ha'daas, Gedolas David).*

The Rebbes of the Lubavitcher dynasty would say additional *Tehillim* in times of distress. "It is a practice that affects the Jewish community in the material sense, in children, life, and livelihood, and in the spiritual sense—with the radiance of blessing, success, salvation and redemption" *(Letter concerning the Rebbe Maharash, 8th of Teves 1936).*

> *A man who had no children spent a lot of money on doctors and medicine. One day the Chazon Ish said to him, "Believe me, sometimes a chapter of Tehillim helps more than medical intervention. Give me your names and I will say Tehillim on your behalf." The Chazon Ish took out a small notebook and wrote down the names of the man and his wife (Ma'aseh Ish).*

> *In 1948 in Yerushalayim, as a group of Jews were davening the evening prayer, bombs began falling. Many members of the minyan fled to bunkers. One boy and his*

friend slipped under the beds and from their hiding place saw the Brisker Rav and his son standing in the corner, saying Tehillim with great passion.

Another eyewitness saw the Brisker Rav put a coin in the pushke of R' Meir Baal Ha'nes during another bombing and start to say Tehillim aloud, word for word. During a crisis he advocated saying Chapter Twenty. He would comment, "We possess diamonds; they are called Tehillim."

The Rebbe Rabbi Shmuel (Maharash) of Lubavitch, son of Rabbi Menachem Mendel (the famed Tzemach Tzedek), occasionally went for a drive in a hansom. The driver would drive the Rebbe through villages near Lubavitch while the Rebbe took in the fresh air, deep in thought.

In one of the villages they passed through, there was a Jewish inn. Usually the Rebbe's carriage passed the inn, but never stopped there. Once, however, in the month of Elul, the Rebbe ordered the driver to halt at the inn.

Alighting from the carriage, the Rebbe entered the living quarters of the innkeeper. There was no one at home except the two boys of the innkeeper.

"Where is your father? Your mother?" the Rebbe asked them.

"They went somewhere, and will soon be back," the boys replied.

"And where is your teacher?"

"Our rebbe has gone home for Rosh Hashanah," was the reply.

The Rebbe Maharash seemed in no hurry to end the conversation. "What has your rebbe taught you?" he asked the boys.

"I've learned Chumash," the older boy replied.

"And I can already read Tehillim," the younger one chirped.

"Shall I test you?" the Rebbe asked. "Bring me a Tehillim."

The boys eagerly went to fetch a Tehillim. The Rebbe opened it at random and invited the boys to read. They began to recite the psalms and the Rebbe recited with them, with much feeling.

Presently the innkeeper's wife returned home. She saw the Rebbe's carriage outside and was greatly surprised and excited, honored by the Rebbe's visit. She entered and remained standing in the kitchen. The voices of her boys blending with that of the Rebbe as they recited the holy words of the psalms enchanted her. Such sweet, heartfelt, soulful prayers she had never heard in all her life! She was particularly moved by the sound of the Rebbe's voice. Although she did not know the meaning of the sacred words, they seemed to penetrate her heart, to touch some spot there, bringing tears to her eyes.

The Tehillim recital came to an end. The Rebbe closed the little book and walked to the door. He stopped at the door, turned to face the boys, and said, "Let us say more Tehillim."

Again their voices lifted as they recited several other psalms in unison. Finally the Rebbe said, "Be well, dear children, and give my regards to your father." He kissed the mezuzah as he walked to the carriage. "Giddyup!" cried the driver, and the carriage rolled away.

The innkeeper's wife remained glued to her place. A strange feeling, a premonition, filled her heart. She felt uneasy and anxious about her husband. He had left that morning to collect debts owed by peasants in the nearby village, and should have been home long ago.

Evening came, with no sign of the innkeeper. Fear gripped the wife. Something must have happened to him! It was near midnight when she heard a knock on the door. How relieved she was to hear her husband call, "Open the door!"

Quickly she unbolted the door. The innkeeper came in, panting heavily, and fell in a swoon. The wife put cold water on his face and shook him until he came to. She helped him to the couch, and soon he felt better. Then he told his wife what had happened.

"I came to a peasant in the nearby village. He owed me a tidy sum of money, having eaten and drunk on credit through the year, saying he would pay at harvest time. The peasant told me to come with him into the barn, where he would measure out some grain in payment of the debt.

"As we entered the barn, he closed the door from the inside, threw a rope around me and tied me to a beam. 'I have no choice but to kill you,' he said.

"I thought he was joking, and told him to stop playing games. But he was in earnest. He began looking for his ax.

"I pleaded with him to spare me. 'Ivan! We've been friends and neighbors for many years. What's gotten into you? I have a wife and children, the same as you. Have you no fear of G-d in your heart? I'll forget the debt; you don't owe me a kopek! Now, be a good fellow, untie me, and we'll have a drink together.'

"He didn't listen to my words, but kept looking for his ax, murmuring, 'What the devil did I do with my ax?' Then he remembered he had been chopping wood behind his hut. So

he left the barn, carefully closing the door from outside.

"Soon afterward the peasant's wife returned home from the field. As she passed the barn, she heard my groaning. She opened the door and saw me tied up. She became frightened and wanted to run out. I pleaded with her to save me.

"The frightened woman said, 'My husband is a murderer; he'll kill me if I interfere with him.' I told her he wouldn't know, and for her own sake and her children's, she should not let her husband commit such a crime. 'Let me loose, and you run back to the field,' I pleaded. 'In the meantime, your husband will sober up, and he will be happy he did not bring such a calamity upon himself and his family.'

"Finally the woman allowed herself to be persuaded. She untied me and returned to the field. I fled to the woods, but was so frightened and sick that I could not run fast, or far. I hid in a haystack.

"I saw from my hiding place that Ivan was running like a madman, ax in hand. He was searching for me. He passed so close to my hiding place, I could smell the whiskey on his breath. He passed me by, ran in circles for a while, until he gave up and went home, disappointed. I lay motionless for a long time, afraid he might return. After dark I crept out of my hiding place and, thank G-d, here I am, safe and sound, G-d be praised."

Then the innkeeper's wife remembered the Rebbe's unexpected and strange visit. She told her husband about it, how the Rebbe had said Tehillim with the children once, and then again.

"It's clear that the Rebbe and children saved my life twice: first in the barn and again in the haystack! This is why the Rebbe said Tehillim twice with our children, bless them."

The innkeeper resolved to recite some chapters of Tehillim every morning after prayers, and to see to it that the boys would also follow this custom. For he was certain that it was in the merit of the Tehillim that he had been saved (Derzeilung fun Tzadikim).

Rav Moshe Finkel, son of the Mirrer Rosh Yeshivah Rav Eliezer Yehuda Finkel, served as a fundraiser for the yeshivah. Although many thousands of dollars passed through his hands on a regular basis, he and his Rebbetzin would not take more than the minimum to cover their bare necessities. Even by the Yerushalmi standards of those days their apartment was considered well below par; with nowhere to hang their clothing, no refrigerator or proper oven.

After paying a visit to Rebbetzin Finkel, the wife of Rav Mordechai Schulman strode purposefully to the home of the Rosh Yeshivah and complained about the sub-standard conditions in his children's apartment. She stated in no uncertain terms, "The Rosh Yeshivah must do all that he is capable of doing to improve the sad state of affairs." Rav Eliezer Yehuda knew that he would never persuade his son to take additional money from the Yeshivah funds.

There was one thing he could do to help his son. He reached for his Tehilim and began to say one chapter after another as his eyes filled with tears. He beseeched Hashem from the depths of his heart, to help his children. After completing his Tehilim he announced to his Rebbitzen, "I have done all that I can do. Now, Hashem will do His share in assisting our children."

A couple of days later, Rav Moshe won a raffle in a sweepstake. He was awarded an apartment in Bat Yam. Rav Moshe sold the apartment and was able to furnish his home in a respectable manner without having to take any money from the Yeshivah.

Rabbi Yitchok Ze'ev Soloveitchik took advantage of cease-fires in 1948 to say Tehillim and encouraged those close to him to do likewise. "If people only knew what could be accomplished by their Tehillim, they would constantly keep a Tehillim at their side. In the World to Come they will tear their hair out for not having said more Tehillim" (Sheal Avicha Ve'Yagedcha).

Three observant Jews manning an Israeli tank and noticed a group of tanks heading toward them—the enemy was approaching!

They rolled into firing position and only then discovered that the cannon's firing mechanism was jammed. The gun would not work. The enemy tanks rolled onward, ever closer. What could they do?

"There is only one thing we can resort to at a time like this," said the first man, and he began reciting Tehillim with great feeling.

To their astonishment, they saw the enemy tanks halt and raise white flags of surrender. Unbelieving, they watched as the turrets opened, and several men emerged. "They're not Arabs!" the men exclaimed. "They're Israelis!"

When their fellow Israelis reached them, they explained the strange circumstances. They had captured the still functioning Arab tanks and were now bringing them to the rear. They had hoped no Israelis would mistake them for the enemy, and had watched nervously as their tank had moved into firing position. Miraculously, the gun had not fired. Both groups of soldiers had been saved through Divine deliverance—helped by the power of Tehillim.

A visitor to the Rebbe of Tchernobel found him saying Tehillim aloud with copious tears. "Surely one of the members of his family is very ill," the visitor thought. "Or perhaps an evil decree has befallen the nation."

Suddenly the Rebbe noticed him and joyfully invited him to enter. When he saw the caller's startled expression, he reassured him. "I am well, and so are the members of my household."

The visitor pressed the Rebbe to tell him why he had recited Tehillim so intensely. The Rebbe explained that a short while ago a Jew had told him of personal problems. "I was so touched that I asked, 'What can I do for this Jew who is in such dire need of Heaven's mercies?' So I took my Tehillim and began to pray."

Parallels to Torah

The *Midrash* cites various parallels between the five books of Moshe and the five books of *Tehillim*. The Torah ends with *Ashrecha Yisrael,* and *Tehillim* begins with *Ashrei Ha'Ish*. King David picks up where *Moshe Rabbeinu* left off *(Yalkut Tehillim 1, 1).*

An early commentary on *Tehillim* elaborates on similarities. There is no chronological order in either Torah or *Tehillim*; there is often no clear connection between one section and another, perhaps to enable the free flow of ideas and the concealment of the Kabbalistic concepts encoded in its holy words *(Mahari Ibn Yachya on Tehillim).* In sweeping statements, Shmuel says that the world was created for *Moshe Rabbeinu, Rav* says that the world was created for *Dovid Hamelech*, and *Rav Yochanan* says for *Moshiach* (*Sanhedrin 98b). Moshe Rabbeinu* established our nation. King David was responsible for our ultimate spiritual development until the evolvement of the end of days (Rabbi S.R. Hirsch, Introduction to *Tehillim*, page 12).

The Rebbe Rashab of Lubavitch said that each time a person finishes *Tehillim* in this world, he is endowed with the ability to understand a new interpretation of *Tehillim* in *Gan Eden (Mipi Hashmuah).*

> *One of the Chabad Rebbes told of a dream: "As I slept, an unfamiliar Rebbe appeared and requested I come with him. We walked at a rapid pace, almost a run, until we arrived at a high mountain. The Rebbe ascended the mountain, but I did not have the strength to follow. The Rebbe advised me to say aloud Torah that I knew by heart, and this enabled me follow my guide.*
>
> *"On the mountain peak was a fortress. Nearby I saw many souls clothed in Shabbos finery. The Rebbe explained that these were souls of Jews who said Tehillim on Hoshana Rabbah. They seemed to dance as one dances on Simchas Torah. Suddenly there was darkness and the sky filled with stars. I was informed that those are the glittering letters of*

Tehillim" (Sefer Hasichos 1936, p. 145).

Rav Shraga Feivel Mendlowitz considered an intimate knowledge of *Tehillim* so valuable that he personally tested *semichah* candidates on difficult passages in *Tehillim (Reb Shraga Feivel, p. 135).*

One day R' Betzalel found Rav Yechezkel Avramsky sitting in front of an open Gemara, crying as he said Tehillim. R' Betzalel asked why he was crying. He explained, "I am crying because I want to understand the words of the Rambam. Many times in the past when this has happened I took my Tehillim in hand, and then succeeded in understanding the Rambam's concepts" (Sheal Avicha Ve'Yagedcha).

Rabbi Yechezkel Avramsky said Tehillim every day, rising early on Shabbos so he could say extra verses. After his release from a Siberian prison he added chapter forty to his routine of daily Tehillim (Peninei Rabeinu Yechezkel).

Musical Merit

The words of *Tehillim* achieve results even if we don't grasp their meaning. As it says in *Tehillim*, "*Lamenatzeach be'neginos al ha'sheminis*—for the chief musician playing on the eight strings." David Ha'Melech was like an expert musician, playing on eight strings. There are many people who cannot play a musical instrument—yet all are capable of winding a music box created by a knowledgeable craftsman. The same is true of *Tehillim*. The psalms do their work on high, even if we are unfamiliar with the meaning of the words. It is enough to simply say the verses that have been formulated by King David, the knowledgeable composer *(Rav Yechiel Meir of Gustenen, known as the "Tehillim Yid")*.

Still, if one wishes to maximize the inherent benefit of the words, one should know their meaning. Those whose *Tehillim* have errors may be accruing sin, not merit *(Peleh Yoetz)*. Rav Chayim Palagi recommended hiring a teacher to instruct one's children in the meaning of the words of the psalms, noting the correlation between comprehension and resolution of our problems *(Introduction to Kol Ha'Kasuv Le'Chayim)*.

Dispelling Decrees

The words of *Tehillim* are able to overcome all negative forces *(Pele Yoetz)*. The Tzemach Tzedek told his sons, "If you could only know the power of verses of *Tehillim* and their effects in the loftiest heights, you would spend every possible moment saying *Tehillim*. Know that *Tehillim* shatters all barriers and rises high without interference, prostrating themselves before the Master of all and bringing about kindness and mercies" *(Excerpt from the diary of R' Yosef Yitchak Schneerson)*.

One Monday, the day after Sukkos, the Tzemach Tzedek

of Lubavitch told his son Reb Boruch Shalom to arrange a minyan to recite the entire book of Tehillim. "No one should know who gave these instructions. It must remain secret," he added.

Starting that Tuesday a minyan gathered early every morning to recite the entire Tehillim. Reb Boruch Shalom and his brothers were filled with trepidation, especially when they heard their father's attendant say that the Rebbe had also been saying many chapters of Tehillim. The Tzemach Tzedek would stop and drop coins into various charity boxes after reciting several verses.

Fifty-three days later, during the week of Vayishlach, the Tzemach Tzedek summoned Reb Shalom and told him to stop the practice. "Those who wish to continue may do so," said the Rebbe, "but I no longer require it to be done."

Three months passed. On the Alter Rebbe's yahrzeit, the Tzemach Tzedek revealed the reason for his strange request earlier that year. On the first night of Rosh Hashanah he had learned of a grave decree made against the Jewish community, a Divine edict that was particularly harsh against Torah students.

"I sought the intervention of my grandfather," continued the Tzemach Tzedek, "but failed. My father-in-law reinforced the gravity of the situation. He revealed that the decree had not been sealed, but warned that publicizing the

matter would be detrimental to the cause.

"Finally during Simchas Torah I envisioned my grandfather. 'Tehillim elevates the person,' the Alter Rebbe said to me. 'Tehillim is the cup of salvation King David wrote for the Jewish nation. Tehillim elevates the soul, quashing all Heavenly accusations. Arrange for the entire Tehillim to be recited secretly for fifty-three consecutive days. This will suppress the Divine decree.'"

The Tzemach Tzedek concluded by describing the incredible effect of Tehillim on high. His sons now realized that the clandestine recital of Tehillim had indeed averted communal tragedy (Tehillim Ohel Yosef Yitzchak).

To some degree, Reb Tzvi Elimelech of Dinov recognized the value of non-Jewish knowledge, following the principle of Chazal that anyone who speaks knowledgeably, even a non-Jew, is called a wise person. But he made distinctions. For example, he would say, "The meteorologists who can predict the weather are using their expertise. But what can they do if they predict a drought, and a Jew says Tehillim with all his heart and is answered favorably? So it is with all their know-how" (Mesharav Esh Lohet vol. 2, p. 163).

In March of 1880, the Rebbe Maharash of Lubavitch

returned from Petersburg deeply distressed. A high-ranking official had proposed new anti-Jewish legislation restricting business activities and making even harsher regulations regarding Jewish residence outside the pale. The Rebbe had traveled to Petersburg and had nearly obtained concessions, including a year's respite before further consideration of the proposals.

But a Senate official, a crony of the vicious anti-Semite who had proposed the new decrees, remained stubborn, and convinced several colleagues to confirm and implement the proposals in full. The Rebbe returned home terribly disturbed, continuing to work on the matter by proxy and through letters.

Later the Rebbe told his son, "Since my stay in Petersburg to deal with the matter of the decrees, I began saying Tehillim even more. Today as I said the verse, 'From every peril he rescued me, and my eye has seen my foes' (Tehillim 54,9), the attendant Bentzion entered. He handed me a telegram that had just arrived, announcing that the Senator had suddenly died. Nevertheless," the Rebbe Maharsh concluded, "I finished reciting the portion of Tehillim" (Letter of Rav Yosef Yitzchak from Otwock Poland 1936).

A woman was in the hospital when victims of a terrorist explosion were brought in by ambulance. One of the injured victims waiting in the emergency room, only lightly wounded, was overheard saying, "What a miracle! What a miracle!" The bystander approached the injured woman, who was clearly not religious, and asked why she said that.

She was told, "This is the second time I was caught in a terrorist attack. Both times those around me were killed, and I was spared. I can only attribute it to the fact that my mother taught us to say Tehillim chapter 34 before ever leaving the house" (Heard from Rebbetzin Zahava Braunstein).

Aid to Teshuva

Tehillim are a handy accessory to *teshuvah*. Rebbe Nachman recommended that whoever wanted to repent completely should recite *Tehillim (Likutei Moharan 2, 73).* Rabbi Yechezkel Shraga Halberstam uncovered a connection in the verse "*Ve'eleh shemos Bnai Yisrael ha'baim mitzrayma.*" The first letters of these words form the word *ha'shavim,* return. The last letters of this verse form the word *Tehillim*—for the two go well together *(Divrey Yechezkel on Shemos).*

When the Rebbe Maharash of Lubavitch was eight years old he entered his father's room. The Tzemach Tzedek was seated at his place studying the Zohar. When the Rebbe's eldest son entered, the Tzemach Tzedek closed his Zohar and remarked, "When the holy saint of Ruzhin says Tehillim, all of Creation is revealed to him. In his Shabbos Tehillim he sees the roots of everything in this world, and he can thus make corrections in the source. Any evil decrees can then be simply nullified." (Excerpted from a letter written by R' Yosef Yitzchak on Tehillim.)

Special Occasions

It is an old custom, received by the *Baal Ha'Tanya* from the *Magid* in the name of his Rebbe the *Baal Shem Tov,* to say the chapter of *Tehillim* that corresponds to the number of one's years after *davening shacharis*. There is also a custom to study every *Rosh Chodesh* the verse (with *Rashi*) from the chapter corresponding to his age *(Letters of Rav Yosef Yitzchak Schneersohn).*

A list of *Tehillim* to be recited on various occasions.

To find a mate	32, 38, 70, 71, 72, 82, 121, 124
For healthy childbirth	4, 5, 8, 20, 35, 57, 93, 108, 142
For recovery from illness	6, 13, 20, 22, 23, 30, 31, 38, 41, 51, 86, 88, 91, 102, 103, 121, 130, 142, 143
For livelihood	23, 34, 36, 62, 67, 85, 104, 121, 136, 144, 145

For thanksgiving	9, 21, 57, 95, 100, 116, 138
For Divine guidance	139
For help in difficult times	20, 38, 85, 86, 102, 130, 142

The *Mateh Ephraim* advises one to say *sefer Tehillim* twice in *Elul*. Why twice? There are one hundred fifty chapters in *Tehillim*. Doubling that number equals three hundred. The numerical equivalent of the Hebrew word *kaper* (atonement) is three hundred.

Many have seen wondrous results from saying *Tehillim* twice without interruption the first night of *Rosh Hashanah*. After completing their second recitation, they say the *Yehi Ratzon* and make their request for children, a mate, livelihood, *shalom bayis*, health, and whatever else they may need *(Hischazkus Be'Tefillah La'Hashem; see Mishnah Berurah end of chapter 582 in the name of Eliyahu Rabah)*.

The Steipler's custom was to complete Tehillim on the two days of Rosh Hashana and again on Yom Kippur (The Steipler, M. Sofer, p. 257).

To hear the Brisker Rav and his sons say Tehillim on Rosh Hashanah was to attain a dramatic lesson in inspiration and dedication. Later he would close himself up in his room and say Tehillim. When he was informed one Shavuos that the Gerrer Rebbe's life was in grave danger, he said nothing, but immediately took his Tehillim and started saying the words with great devotion (Uvdos ve'Hanhagos Le'Bais Brisk).

Devotion and Tears

Saying *Tehillim* with tears cleanses the vessel *(Igros Kodesh of Rav Yosef Yitzchak, p. 390).*

Rav Shmuel Binyomin Sofer, the Ksav Sofer, went to Budapest for a vital meeting. He was accompanied by his student Rabbi Eliezer Grunwald, the Arugas Habosem.

After settling into their hotel room, the Ksav Sofer advised his disciple to take a walk and get some fresh air. He followed his Rebbe's advice, but after a short walk felt he had fulfilled his obligation and returned so he could observe his Rebbe's preparations for the gathering that had brought them to the capital.

Through a window he saw his Rebbe crying bitterly. When the Ksav Sofer noticed that he was being observed, he called his student into the room.

"Now that you have seen my devotions, why should I hide anything from you? My dear disciple, the Jewish people

require great compassion. Join me as I say Tehillim."

The two began saying Tehillim with great devotion. For six hours they said Tehillim with hot tears running down their cheeks. Years later the Arugas Habosem was heard saying, "If only I could merit once again to feel that spiritual elevation I experienced when I said Tehillim in Budapest together with my Rebbe" (Introduction to Tehillim Tehilah Ve'Tiferes).

When the Chofetz Chaim was given his mother's Tehillim, he became very emotional and began to cry. He explained, "Do you have any idea how many tears my mother shed over this Tehillim, beseeching Hashem that her son should become a genuine Jew?" (Le'Shichno Tidrishu)

Rabbi Michoel Levy, a school principal from Brooklyn, went to visit the renowned dayan Rabbi Yisroel Grossman at his home in the old Batei Varshaw section of Jerusalem. Despite the late hour, he was enthusiastically greeted by both Rabbi Yisroel and his rebbetzin when he arrived. The men sat at the table, and the rebbetzin offered Rabbi Levy a cup of tea. Despite Rabbi Levy's protests, the rebbetzin insisted on serving him tea.

The rebbetzin looked at her visitor and said in Yiddish, "There are two things that can never hurt a Yid. Ah glezeleh tay (a glass of tea) und a kapitel Tehillim (and the recitation of a chapter of Psalms). Uber baida darfen zain varehm! (But both have to be warm!)" Tehillim said with warmth and enthusiasm can be very effective (The Maggid Speaks, Rabbi P. Krohn).

Reciting the Whole

Rabbi Meshulam Zusya Twersky of Chernobyl stressed saying the entire book of *Tehillim* to protect a person from harm. He often quoted the interpretation of his ancestor Rav Zusya of Anipoli on the verse, "*Mi yemalel gevuros Hashem, yashmia kol tehillaso.*" He explained, "If a person wants to cut (*yemalel* can mean destroying and cutting) the *gevuros* (Hashem's quality of strict judgment) he should say the whole of *Tehillim.*"

One evening R' Yosef Chaim Sonnenfeld rose for Tikun Chatzos. Instead of the regular prayers, he took a Tehillim and began praying with fearsome emotion.

Next day his son R' Mordechai returned from a business trip, telling of dangers he had encountered the previous evening on his way home. They soon determined that it was at that very same time his father was saying Tehillim on his behalf (Marah De'Arah Yisrael).

R' Ben Zion Shapira always said that one needing salvation should say *Tehillim* each day, according to the recommendation of the *Peleh Yoetz* (*Tzvi La'Tzaddik*).

A follower of Rabbi Meshulam Zusya Twersky arranged to travel to South Africa to act as a chazan during the Yomim Noraim. He came to bid farewell to Rav Meshulam Zusya, who reiterated how reciting all of Tehillim can help even when all hope is lost. He mentioned that he himself succeeded in escaping from Russia because of his custom of saying the whole book of Tehillim without pause.

"Why is he telling me all this now?" the chassid asked himself.

Later in Johannesburg, the chassid was walking down a street when someone ran out of a house and begged him to come inside. "There's a Jew dying here," the man gasped. "You look like a rabbi, with your long beard. Perhaps you can say his confession with him."

"Certainly," agreed the chassid.

Inside the house the chassid found a dying man in bed, surrounded by his children. He suddenly remembered the Rebbe's parting advice.

"Hurry," he told the man's family. "Bring three more Jews here so we have a minyan and we'll say the whole of Tehillim

together. I have heard it can save a person's life."

Three men were rounded up. It turned out the sick man's sons could not read Hebrew. The chassid patiently recited every word of the Tehillim, while they repeated it. This painstaking recitation took six hours. Soon afterward the man showed signs of recovery, and he eventually regained his health (Yated Ne'eman).

The author of the *Peleh Yoetz* says that even great scholars should study the book of *Tehillim* with a weekly group. He writes, "One who wishes to cling to Hashem and His praises should cling to the study of *Tehillim.* It is a tradition among the great and holy men that anyone who has any pressing hardship or pain, or is traveling on the road or passing through oceans and rivers, should read the entire Book of *Tehillim* without interruption, with proper concentration, devotion and humility—and he will behold wonders. This is tried and true protection."

Rebbe David of Tolna said to his brother Rebbe Yitzchak of Square, "I heard that you complete the entire book of Tehillim daily. I say a little, and I cannot continue for I feel I am going to expire."

Rebbe Yitzchak replied, "That is the way Tehillim should be said, but one should carry on" (Ha'osher Sheb'tefillah).

Rebbe Moshe Tzvi of Savoran said that saying *Tehillim*

without interruption referred to no disruption between the mouth and heart. If the two worked together, then one was guaranteed that his desire would be fulfilled (*Ibid*).

Rav Ben Zion Avraham Schapiro said Tehillim at the Kosel regularly. Spiritual giants who watched his attentive prayers were deeply moved. When Rav Ben Zion was asked to daven for a sick person, he would take his Tehillim and begin to recite the entire sefer, from beginning to end. When the Minchas Eluzar, the Munkatcher Rebbe, asked him to daven for one of his childless chassidim, he davened Shacharis at the Kosel for forty consecutive days, completing the book of Tehillim after his prayers (Tzvi Le'Tzaddik).

About the Author

A former student of Rebbetzin Vichna Kaplan, Sarah Feldbrand served as principal of Ohel Sorah Seminary of Montreal and is also the founder of the Jewish Heritage Program in Montreal. She is the author of *Middos, Towards Meaningful Prayer Volume I, From Sarah to Sarah, and In Search of Rabbi Levi Yitzchak.*